HEADNOTE

Welcome to the "Perfect Ninja CREAMi Cookbook: +180 Beginner-Friendly Recipes for Gourmet Frozen Desserts. Light Ice Creams, Smoothies, Gelato, Milkshakes, Sorbets, and Other Options. Includes Nutritional Information." As a professional chef with many years of experience in American frozen dessert cuisine, it brings me immense joy to introduce you to this delightful journey of creating your own frozen treats at home.

Ice cream has always held a special place in American hearts. From the childhood excitement of a scoop on a hot summer day to the sophisticated pleasure of savoring a well-crafted gelato, frozen desserts are a beloved part of our culinary landscape. However, making these delicious treats at home often seemed like a daunting task—until now.

The Ninja CREAMi has revolutionized home dessert making, and this cookbook is your ultimate guide to unlocking its full potential. With over 180 beginner-friendly recipes, this book is designed to make your dessert-making experience fun, easy, and incredibly rewarding. Whether you're new to the kitchen or a seasoned home chef, you'll find recipes that cater to every taste and occasion.

There's something incredibly satisfying about creating your own frozen desserts. It's not just about the end product; it's about the joy of the process, the creativity involved, and the smiles it brings to those you share it with. The "Perfect Ninja CREAMi Cookbook" is designed to be your companion on this delicious journey, providing you with the tools and inspiration you need to create delightful treats for any occasion.

The variety of recipes ensures that you'll never run out of new and exciting flavors to try.

Embrace the Joy of Homemade Frozen Desserts!

Overview of the Ninja Creami Ice Cream Maker

- **Versatility:** The Ninja Creami is not just an ice cream maker; it's a multi-functional kitchen appliance that can also make frozen yogurt, gelato, sorbet, and various other frozen treats. This versatility makes it appealing to users who enjoy experimenting with different dessert recipes.

- **Variety of Settings:** It typically comes with multiple settings and pre-programmed modes for different types of frozen desserts. These settings ensure that you can achieve the desired consistency and texture for your ice cream or other treats.

- **Capacity:** The Ninja Creami usually comes in different sizes, with varying capacities to suit different needs. Whether you're making a small batch for yourself or a larger one for a gathering, there's likely a size that fits your requirements.

- **Ease of Use:** Many users appreciate how easy it is to use the Ninja Creami. It often features intuitive controls and a straightforward process for making ice cream and other frozen treats. Some models may also come with recipe books or online resources to help you get started.

- **Fast Freezing:** One of the key features of the Ninja Creami is its ability to freeze ingredients quickly, allowing you to enjoy your homemade treats in a relatively short amount of time compared to traditional ice cream makers.

- **Cleaning:** Depending on the model, the Ninja Creami may have dishwasher-safe parts, making cleanup a breeze after you've finished making your desserts.

- **Design:** The design of the Ninja Creami is often sleek and modern, fitting well into most kitchen aesthetics. Its compact size also makes it easy to store when not in use.

The Art of Ice Cream Making

- **Ingredients:** The foundation of any good ice cream is its ingredients. Typically, these include cream, milk, sugar, and flavorings such as vanilla extract or fruit purees. High-quality ingredients can significantly impact the final taste and texture of the ice cream.

- **Balance of Ingredients:** Achieving the perfect balance of ingredients is crucial. The ratio of cream to milk affects the richness and creaminess of the ice cream, while the amount of sugar impacts sweetness and texture. Balancing these elements ensures a harmonious flavor and a smooth, creamy texture.

- **Flavor Development:** Ice cream making allows for endless flavor possibilities. Whether you're using fresh fruits, nuts, chocolates, spices, or other ingredients, the key is to balance flavors and create a well-rounded taste profile. Experimenting with different combinations can lead to unique and delicious creations.

- **Texture:** Texture is a hallmark of great ice cream. Achieving the ideal texture involves careful control of temperature and churning. Properly incorporating air into the mixture through churning creates a light and creamy texture, while preventing the formation of ice crystals ensures a smooth mouthfeel.

- **Churning:** Churning is the process of agitating the ice cream mixture while it freezes, which helps incorporate air and prevent the formation of large ice crystals. The duration and speed of churning can vary depending on the desired consistency and texture of the ice cream.

- **Temperature Control:** Temperature control is critical throughout the ice cream making process. Freezing the mixture at the right temperature ensures proper crystallization and texture development, while allowing the ice cream to temper slightly before serving enhances its scoopability and creaminess.

- **Presentation:** Presentation is the final touch in the art of ice cream making. Whether you're scooping it into cones, bowls, or creating elaborate sundaes, attention to detail can elevate the overall experience. Garnishes, sauces, and toppings add visual appeal and additional layers of flavor and texture.

- **Creativity and Innovation:** The art of ice cream making encourages creativity and innovation. From classic flavors to avant-garde combinations, there's always room for experimentation and pushing the boundaries of traditional techniques to create something truly unique and memorable.

Tips and Tricks for Perfect Ice Cream

- **Use Quality Ingredients:** Start with fresh, high-quality ingredients for the best flavor and texture. Use full-fat dairy for richness and creaminess.
- **Pre-Chill Ingredients:** Before churning, make sure your ice cream base is well chilled. This helps it freeze faster and churn more efficiently.
- **Don't Overheat the Base:** When making the base, heat it gently and avoid boiling. Overheating can result in a grainy texture or curdled appearance.
- **Properly Temper Eggs:** If your recipe calls for eggs, temper them slowly with the hot milk mixture to prevent them from scrambling.
- **Add Flavorings Carefully:** If using flavorings like extracts or alcohol, add them sparingly to avoid overpowering the base. Taste as you go and adjust accordingly.
- **Chill the Churner:** Before churning, chill your ice cream maker's bowl in the freezer overnight. A colder bowl leads to faster freezing and smoother ice cream.
- **Churn Until Just Right:** Pay attention to the consistency of the ice cream as it churns. It should be thick and creamy, with a soft-serve texture. Avoid over-churning, which can result in a grainy or icy texture.
- **Mix-Ins at the Right Time:** If adding mix-ins like nuts or chocolate chips, add them towards the end of churning to evenly distribute them without crushing or sinking.
- **Freeze Properly:** Transfer the churned ice cream to a freezer-safe container and press a piece of plastic wrap directly onto the surface to prevent ice crystals from forming. Seal tightly with a lid and freeze until firm.
- **Aging Improves Flavor:** Allow the ice cream to "age" in the freezer for a few hours or overnight before serving. This allows the flavors to meld and the texture to stabilize.
- **Serve with Style:** For an extra special touch, serve your ice cream in chilled bowls or cones. Garnish with complementary toppings like fresh fruit, chocolate shavings, or a drizzle of caramel sauce.
- **Clean Your Equipment:** Properly clean and dry your ice cream maker after each use to prevent off-flavors and maintain performance.

Table of Content

Ice Cream

- Strawberry Swirl Ice Cream — 1
- Mint Chocolate Chip Ice Cream — 1
- Caramel Macchiato Ice Cream — 2
- Coffee Crunch Ice Cream — 2
- Peanut Butter Cup Ice Cream — 3
- Rocky Road Ice Cream — 3
- Coconut Almond Ice Cream — 4
- Birthday Cake Ice Cream — 4
- Pistachio Ice Cream — 5
- Pineapple Coconut — 5
- Salted Caramel Ice Cream — 6
- Cookie Dough Ice Cream — 6
- Cherry Garcia Ice Cream — 7
- Butter Pecan Ice Cream — 7
- Blueberry Cheesecake Ice Cream — 8
- Chocolate Hazelnut Ice Cream — 8
- Lemon Sorbet Ice Cream — 9
- Raspberry Ripple Ice Cream — 9
- Mocha Almond Fudge Ice Cream — 10
- Maple Walnut Ice Cream — 10
- Red Velvet Ice Cream — 11
- Banana Nut Ice Cream — 11
- Key Lime Pie Ice Cream — 12
- Orange Creamsicle Ice Cream — 12
- Peppermint Stick Ice Cream — 13
- Almond Joy Ice Cream — 13
- Honey Lavender Ice Cream — 14
- Blueberry Lemonade — 14
- S'mores Ice Cream — 15
- Cotton Candy Ice Cream — 15
- Chocolate Coconut Ice Cream — 16
- Peanut Butter Banana Ice Cream — 16
- Black Forest Ice Cream — 17
- White Chocolate Raspberry Ice Cream — 17
- Cinnamon Roll Ice Cream — 18
- Mango Tango Ice Cream — 18

Light Ice Cream

- Strawberry Shortcake Light Ice Cream — 19
- Mint Chocolate Chip Light Ice Cream — 19
- Cookies and Cream Light Ice Cream — 20
- Coffee Toffee Light Ice Cream — 20
- Peanut Butter Swirl Light Ice Cream — 21
- Rocky Road Light Ice Cream — 21
- Coconut Almond Joy Light Ice Cream — 22
- Birthday Cake Light Ice Cream — 22
- Pistachio Light Ice Cream — 23
- Neapolitan Light Ice Cream — 23
- Salted Caramel Light Ice Cream — 24
- Chocolate Brownie Light Ice Cream — 24
- Cherry Vanilla Light Ice Cream — 25
- Blueberry Cheesecake Light Ice Cream — 25
- Lemon Sorbet Light Ice Cream — 26
- Raspberry Swirl Light Ice Cream — 26
- Mocha Almond Fudge Light Ice Cream — 27
- Maple Walnut Light Ice Cream — 27
- Peppermint Stick Light Ice Cream — 28
- Orange Creamsicle Light Ice Cream — 28

Sorbet

- Lemon Sorbet — 29
- Raspberry Sorbet — 29
- Strawberry Sorbet — 30
- Mango Sorbet — 30
- Pineapple Sorbet — 31
- Watermelon Sorbet — 31

Table of Content

- Blueberry Sorbet — 32
- Peach Sorbet — 32
- Kiwi Sorbet — 33
- Passionfruit Sorbet — 33
- Lime Sorbet — 34
- Orange Sorbet — 34
- Grapefruit Sorbet — 35
- Coconut Sorbet — 35
- Blackberry Sorbet — 36
- Cranberry Sorbet — 36
- Cherry Sorbet — 37
- Green Apple Sorbet — 37
- Pear Sorbet — 38
- Papaya Sorbet — 38
- Lychee Sorbet — 39
- Guava Sorbet — 39
- Plum Sorbet — 40
- Apricot Sorbet — 40
- Banana Sorbet — 41
- Fig Sorbet — 41
- Honeydew Melon Sorbet — 42
- Cantaloupe Sorbet — 42
- Tangerine Sorbet — 43
- Mango-Passionfruit Sorbet — 43
- Raspberry-Lime Sorbet — 44
- Pomegranate Sorbet — 44

Gelato

- Vanilla Bean Gelato — 45
- Chocolate Gelato — 45
- Stracciatella Gelato — 46
- Hazelnut Gelato — 46
- Pistachio Gelato — 47
- Espresso Gelato — 47
- Key Lime Pie Gelato — 48
- Cookies and Cream Gelato — 48
- Mint Chocolate Chip Gelato — 49
- Almond Gelato — 49
- Coconut Gelato — 50
- Salted Caramel Gelato — 50
- Raspberry Ripple Gelato — 51
- Lemon Sorbetto Gelato — 51
- Mango Sorbetto Gelato — 52
- Strawberry Sorbetto Gelato — 52
- Pistachio Almond Gelato — 53
- Dark Chocolate Gelato — 53
- White Chocolate Raspberry Gelato — 54
- Caramel Macchiato Gelato — 54
- Amaretto Gelato — 55
- Cherry Chocolate Gelato — 55
- Peanut Butter Cup Gelato — 56
- Banana Nutella Gelato — 56
- Blueberry Cheesecake Gelato — 57
- Honey Lavender Gelato — 57
- Orange Creamsicle Gelato — 58
- Coconut Lime Gelato — 58
- Black Forest Gelato — 59
- Mango Tango Gelato — 59
- Pineapple Coconut Gelato — 60
- Cinnamon Roll Gelato — 60

Smoothie Bowl

- Mixed Berry Smoothie Bowl — 61
- Tropical Mango Smoothie Bowl — 61
- Strawberry Banana Smoothie Bowl — 62
- Blueberry Acai Smoothie Bowl — 62

Table of Content

- Peanut Butter Banana Smoothie Bowl — 63
- Green Goddess Smoothie Bowl — 63
- Chocolate Peanut Butter Smoothie Bowl — 64
- Peach Raspberry Smoothie Bowl — 64
- Kiwi Coconut Smoothie Bowl — 65
- Pineapple Spinach Smoothie Bowl — 65
- Cherry Almond Smoothie Bowl — 66
- Watermelon Mint Smoothie Bowl — 66
- Raspberry Lime Smoothie Bowl — 67
- Mango Pineapple Smoothie Bowl — 67
- Dragon Fruit Smoothie Bowl — 68
- Orange Carrot Smoothie Bowl — 68
- Beet Berry Smoothie Bowl — 69
- Avocado Blueberry Smoothie Bowl — 69
- Blackberry Banana Smoothie Bowl — 70
- Strawberry Kiwi Smoothie Bowl — 70
- Raspberry Peach Smoothie Bowl — 71
- Chocolate Cherry Smoothie Bowl — 71
- Apple Cinnamon Smoothie Bowl — 72
- Pina Colada Smoothie Bowl — 72
- Mixed Fruit Smoothie Bowl — 73
- Cranberry Orange Smoothie Bowl — 73

Milkshake

- Classic Vanilla Milkshake — 74
- Rich Chocolate Milkshake — 74
- Strawberry Milkshake — 75
- Cookies and Cream Milkshake — 75
- Mint Chocolate Chip Milkshake — 76
- Peanut Butter Cup Milkshake — 76
- Banana Split Milkshake — 77
- Salted Caramel Milkshake — 77
- Chocolate Peanut Butter Milkshake — 78
- Oreo Milkshake — 78
- Coconut Milkshake — 79
- Coffee Milkshake — 79
- Blueberry Milkshake — 80
- Peach Milkshake — 80
- Raspberry Milkshake — 81
- Cherry Milkshake — 81
- Nutella Milkshake — 82
- Almond Joy Milkshake — 82
- Mocha Milkshake — 83
- Caramel Macchiato Milkshake — 83
- Key Lime Pie Milkshake — 84
- Pineapple Coconut Milkshake — 84
- Mango Milkshake — 85
- Blackberry Milkshake — 85

Mix-in — 86-87-88

Strawberry Swirl Ice Cream

 Serves: 8 ; Prep: 30 Min

Ingredient

- 300g fresh strawberries, hulled and chopped
- 100g granulated sugar
- 1 tablespoon lemon juice
- 300ml double cream
- 150ml whole milk

Per Serving:

Calories: 220; Fat: 16g;
Carbohydrates: 18g; Protein: 2g

Instruction:

1. In a blender, puree the strawberries until smooth.
2. In a saucepan, combine the strawberry puree, granulated sugar, and lemon juice. Cook over medium heat, stirring constantly, until the sugar is dissolved and the mixture is slightly thickened, about 5 minutes. Remove from heat and let it cool completely.
3. In a large mixing bowl, whisk together the double cream and whole milk until well combined.
4. Pour the strawberry mixture into the cream mixture and gently fold until fully incorporated.
5. Pour the base into an empty tub. Place the lid on the tub and freeze for 24 hours.
6. Remove tub from freezer and remove lid from tub. Please use the Quick Start Guide for assembly and processing information.
7. Select ICE CREAM.
8. Once processing is complete, add mix-ins or remove ice cream from tub and serve immediately.

CHAPTER 01: ICE CREAM

Mint Chocolate Chip Ice Cream

 Serves: 6 ; Prep: 15 Min

Ingredient

- 300ml double cream
- 150ml whole milk
- 100g granulated sugar
- 1 teaspoon peppermint extract
- Green food coloring (optional)
- 100g dark chocolate, chopped into small chunks

Per Serving:

Calories: 280; Fat: 20g;
Carbohydrates: 22g; Protein: 3g

Instruction:

1. In a large mixing bowl, whisk together the double cream, whole milk, granulated sugar, and peppermint extract until well combined.
2. Add a few drops of green food coloring, if desired, and mix until evenly distributed.
3. Pour the mixture into the Ninja CREAMi tub.
4. Place the lid on the tub and freeze for 24 hours.
5. Remove the tub from the freezer and remove the lid.
6. Use the Quick Start Guide for assembly and processing instructions.
7. Select ICE CREAM program on the Ninja CREAMi.
8. Once processing is complete, add the chopped dark chocolate chunks during the last few minutes of churning.
9. Once the ice cream is ready, scoop it into serving bowls and enjoy immediately.

Caramel Macchiato Ice Cream

 Serves: 6 ; Prep: 20 Min

Ingredient

- 250ml double cream
- 250ml whole milk
- 100g granulated sugar
- 2 tablespoons instant coffee granules
- 2 tablespoons caramel sauce
- 50g dark chocolate, chopped (optional)

Per Serving:

Calories: 280; Fat: 18g;
Carbohydrates: 28g; Protein: 3g

Instruction:

1. In a saucepan, heat the double cream and whole milk over medium heat until warm but not boiling.
2. Stir in the granulated sugar and instant coffee granules until dissolved.
3. Remove from heat and let it cool to room temperature.
4. Once cooled, stir in the caramel sauce until well combined.
5. Pour the mixture into the Ninja CREAMi tub.
6. Place the lid on the tub and freeze for 24 hours.
7. Remove the tub from the freezer and remove the lid.
8. Use the Quick Start Guide for assembly and processing instructions.
9. Select ICE CREAM program on the Ninja CREAMi.
10. Once processing is complete, add the chopped dark chocolate (if using) during the last few minutes of churning.
11. Once the ice cream is ready, scoop it into serving bowls and enjoy immediately.

CHAPTER 01: ICE CREAM

Coffee Crunch Ice Cream

 Serves: 6 ; Prep: 20 Min

Ingredient

- 250ml double cream
- 250ml whole milk
- 80g granulated sugar
- 2 tablespoons instant coffee granules
- 50g chocolate-covered coffee beans, roughly chopped

Per Serving:

Calories: 240; Fat: 16g;
Carbohydrates: 21g; Protein: 3g

Instruction:

1. In a saucepan, heat the double cream and whole milk over medium heat until warm but not boiling.
2. Stir in the granulated sugar and instant coffee granules until dissolved.
3. Remove from heat and let it cool to room temperature.
4. Pour the mixture into the Ninja CREAMi tub.
5. Place the lid on the tub and freeze for 24 hours.
6. Remove the tub from the freezer and remove the lid.
7. Use the Quick Start Guide for assembly and processing instructions.
8. Select ICE CREAM program on the Ninja CREAMi.
9. Once processing is complete, add the chopped chocolate-covered coffee beans during the last few minutes of churning.
10. Once the ice cream is ready, scoop it into serving bowls and enjoy immediately.

Peanut Butter Cup Ice Cream

 Serves: 6 ; Prep: 20 Min

Ingredient

- 250ml double cream
- 250ml whole milk
- 80g granulated sugar
- 80g smooth peanut butter
- 100g chocolate chips or chopped chocolate

Per Serving:

Calories: 280; Fat: 20g;
Carbohydrates: 22g; Protein: 5g

Instruction:

1. In a saucepan, heat the double cream and whole milk over medium heat until warm but not boiling.
2. Stir in the granulated sugar until dissolved.
3. Remove from heat and let it cool slightly.
4. In a separate bowl, microwave the peanut butter for 20-30 seconds until soft and smooth.
5. Stir the peanut butter into the warm cream mixture until fully incorporated.
6. Pour the mixture into the Ninja CREAMi tub.
7. Place the lid on the tub and freeze for 24 hours.
8. Remove the tub from the freezer and remove the lid.
9. Use the Quick Start Guide for assembly and processing instructions.
10. Select ICE CREAM program on the Ninja CREAMi.
11. Once processing is complete, add the chocolate chips or chopped chocolate during the last few minutes of churning.
12. Once the ice cream is ready, scoop it into serving bowls and enjoy immediately.

CHAPTER 01: ICE CREAM

Rocky Road Ice Cream

 Serves: 6 ; Prep: 20 Min

Ingredient

- 250ml double cream
- 250ml whole milk
- 80g granulated sugar
- 50g dark chocolate, chopped
- 50g milk chocolate, chopped
- 50g mini marshmallows
- 50g chopped almonds

Per Serving:

Calories: 290; Fat: 20g;
Carbohydrates: 25g; Protein: 4g

Instruction:

1. In a saucepan, heat the double cream and whole milk over medium heat until warm but not boiling.
2. Stir in the granulated sugar until dissolved.
3. Remove from heat and let it cool slightly.
4. Pour the mixture into the Ninja CREAMi tub.
5. Place the lid on the tub and freeze for 24 hours.
6. Remove the tub from the freezer and remove the lid.
7. Use the Quick Start Guide for assembly and processing instructions.
8. Select ICE CREAM program on the Ninja CREAMi.
9. Once processing is complete, add the chopped dark chocolate, milk chocolate, mini marshmallows, and chopped almonds during the last few minutes of churning.
10. Once the ice cream is ready, scoop it into serving bowls and enjoy immediately.

Coconut Almond Ice Cream

 Serves: 6 ; Prep: 15 Min

Ingredient

- 250ml double cream
- 250ml whole milk
- 80g granulated sugar
- 50g shredded coconut
- 50g chopped almonds

 **Instruction:**

1. In a saucepan, heat the double cream and whole milk over medium heat until warm but not boiling.
2. Stir in the granulated sugar until dissolved.
3. Remove from heat and let it cool slightly.
4. Stir in the shredded coconut and chopped almonds until well combined.
5. Pour the mixture into the Ninja CREAMi tub.
6. Place the lid on the tub and freeze for 24 hours.
7. Remove the tub from the freezer and remove the lid.
8. Use the Quick Start Guide for assembly and processing instructions.
9. Select ICE CREAM program on the Ninja CREAMi.
10. Once processing is complete, scoop the ice cream into serving bowls and enjoy immediately.

<u>Per Serving:</u>

Calories: 280; Fat: 20g;
Carbohydrates: 22g; Protein: 3g

CHAPTER 01: ICE CREAM

Birthday Cake Ice Cream

 Serves: 6 ; Prep: 15 Min

Ingredient

- 250ml double cream
- 250ml whole milk
- 80g granulated sugar
- 1 teaspoon vanilla extract
- 50g rainbow sprinkles
- 50g crushed vanilla sponge cake or cake mix

Instruction:

1. In a saucepan, heat the double cream and whole milk over medium heat until warm but not boiling.
2. Stir in the granulated sugar and vanilla extract until dissolved.
3. Remove from heat and let it cool slightly.
4. Stir in the rainbow sprinkles and crushed vanilla sponge cake until well combined.
5. Pour the mixture into the Ninja CREAMi tub.
6. Place the lid on the tub and freeze for 24 hours.
7. Remove the tub from the freezer and remove the lid.
8. Use the Quick Start Guide for assembly and processing instructions.
9. Select ICE CREAM program on the Ninja CREAMi.
10. Once processing is complete, scoop the ice cream into serving bowls and enjoy immediately.

<u>Per Serving:</u>

Calories: 290; Fat: 20g;
Carbohydrates: 24g; Protein: 3g

Pistachio Ice Cream

 Serves: 6 ; Prep: 15 Min

Ingredient

- 250ml double cream
- 250ml whole milk
- 80g granulated sugar
- 1 teaspoon almond extract
- 70g shelled pistachios, finely chopped

 Instruction:

1. In a saucepan, heat the double cream and whole milk over medium heat until warm but not boiling.
2. Stir in the granulated sugar and almond extract until dissolved.
3. Remove from heat and let it cool slightly.
4. Stir in the finely chopped pistachios until well combined.
5. Pour the mixture into the Ninja CREAMi tub.
6. Place the lid on the tub and freeze for 24 hours.
7. Remove the tub from the freezer and remove the lid.
8. Use the Quick Start Guide for assembly and processing instructions.
9. Select ICE CREAM program on the Ninja CREAMi.
10. Once processing is complete, scoop the ice cream into serving bowls and enjoy immediately.

Per Serving:

Calories: 260; Fat: 18g;
Carbohydrates: 22g; Protein: 4g

CHAPTER 01: ICE CREAM

Pineapple Coconut

 Serves: 6 ; Prep: 10 Min

Ingredient

- 250ml double cream
- 250ml coconut milk
- 80g granulated sugar
- 200g pineapple chunks, canned or fresh

Instruction:

1. In a blender, combine the double cream, coconut milk, and granulated sugar. Blend until smooth.
2. Add the pineapple chunks to the blender and blend until the mixture is well combined and smooth.
3. Pour the mixture into the Ninja CREAMi tub.
4. Place the lid on the tub and freeze for 24 hours.
5. Remove the tub from the freezer and remove the lid.
6. Use the Quick Start Guide for assembly and processing instructions.
7. Select ICE CREAM program on the Ninja CREAMi.
8. Once processing is complete, scoop the Pineapple Coconut ice cream into serving bowls and enjoy immediately.

Per Serving:

Calories: 250; Fat: 18g;
Carbohydrates: 22g; Protein: 2g

Salted Caramel Ice Cream

 Serves: 6 ; Prep: 20 Min

Ingredient

- 250ml double cream
- 250ml whole milk
- 100g granulated sugar
- 2 tablespoons water
- 1 teaspoon sea salt flakes

Per Serving:

Calories: 280; Fat: 20g; Carbohydrates: 25g; Protein: 3g

 Instruction:

1. In a saucepan, heat the double cream and whole milk over medium heat until warm but not boiling.
2. In a separate saucepan, combine the granulated sugar and water. Heat over medium-high heat, stirring constantly until the sugar dissolves.
3. Allow the sugar mixture to boil without stirring until it turns a deep amber color, about 5-7 minutes.
4. Remove the caramel from heat and slowly pour in the warm cream mixture while stirring constantly. Be careful as it may splatter.
5. Stir in the sea salt flakes until well combined.
6. Allow the caramel mixture to cool slightly.
7. Pour the caramel mixture into the Ninja CREAMi tub.
8. Place the lid on the tub and freeze for 24 hours.
9. Remove the tub from the freezer and remove the lid.
10. Use the Quick Start Guide for assembly and processing instructions.
11. Select ICE CREAM program on the Ninja CREAMi.
12. Once processing is complete, scoop the Salted Caramel ice cream into serving bowls and enjoy immediately.

CHAPTER 01: ICE CREAM

Cookie Dough Ice Cream

 Serves: 6 ; Prep: 10 Min

Ingredient

- 250ml double cream
- 250ml whole milk
- 100g granulated sugar
- 1 teaspoon vanilla extract
- 100g cookie dough pieces (store-bought or homemade)

Per Serving:

Calories: 280; Fat: 18g; Carbohydrates: 25g; Protein: 4g

Instruction:

1. In a bowl, combine the double cream, whole milk, granulated sugar, and vanilla extract. Mix until the sugar is dissolved.
2. Pour the mixture into the Ninja CREAMi tub.
3. Add the cookie dough pieces into the tub.
4. Place the lid on the tub and freeze for 24 hours.
5. Remove the tub from the freezer and remove the lid.
6. Use the Quick Start Guide for assembly and processing instructions.
7. Select ICE CREAM program on the Ninja CREAMi.
8. Once processing is complete, scoop the Cookie Dough ice cream into serving bowls and enjoy immediately.

Cherry Garcia Ice Cream

 Serves: 6 ; Prep: 10 Min

Ingredient

- 250ml double cream
- 250ml whole milk
- 100g cherries, pitted and chopped
- 50g chocolate chunks or chips

 **Instruction:**

1. In a bowl, combine the double cream and whole milk. Mix well.
2. Pour the mixture into the Ninja CREAMi tub.
3. Add the chopped cherries and chocolate chunks into the tub.
4. Place the lid on the tub and freeze for 24 hours.
5. Remove the tub from the freezer and remove the lid.
6. Use the Quick Start Guide for assembly and processing instructions.
7. Select ICE CREAM program on the Ninja CREAMi.
8. Once processing is complete, scoop the Cherry Garcia ice cream into serving bowls and enjoy immediately.

Per Serving:

Calories: 280; Fat: 20g;
Carbohydrates: 22g; Protein: 4g

CHAPTER 01: ICE CREAM

Butter Pecan Ice Cream

 Serves: 6 ; Prep: 15 Min

Ingredient

- 200ml double cream
- 200ml whole milk
- 100g pecans, chopped
- 50g butter
- 50g brown sugar
- 1 teaspoon vanilla extract

Instruction:

1. In a pan over medium heat, melt the butter.
2. Add the chopped pecans and brown sugar to the melted butter. Cook, stirring constantly, until the sugar is dissolved and the pecans are coated, about 3-4 minutes. Remove from heat and let cool.
3. In a bowl, combine the double cream, whole milk, and vanilla extract. Mix well.
4. Pour the mixture into the Ninja CREAMi tub.
5. Add the cooled pecan mixture into the tub.
6. Place the lid on the tub and freeze for 24 hours.
7. Remove the tub from the freezer and remove the lid.
8. Use the Quick Start Guide for assembly and processing instructions.
9. Select ICE CREAM program on the Ninja CREAMi.
10. Once processing is complete, scoop the Butter Pecan ice cream into serving bowls and enjoy immediately.

Per Serving:

Calories: 260; Fat: 21g;
Carbohydrates: 16g; Protein: 3g

Blueberry Cheesecake Ice Cream

 Serves: 6 ; Prep: 15 Min

Ingredient

- 200ml double cream
- 200ml whole milk
- 100g cream cheese, softened
- 50g caster sugar
- 100g fresh blueberries
- 50g crushed digestive biscuits

Per Serving:

Calories: 180; Fat: 12g;
Carbohydrates: 15g; Protein: 2g

 Instruction:

1. In a blender, combine the cream cheese, caster sugar, and fresh blueberries. Blend until smooth.
2. In a separate bowl, mix the double cream and whole milk.
3. Pour the cream mixture into the blender with the blueberry mixture. Blend until well combined.
4. Pour the base into the Ninja CREAMi tub.
5. Add the crushed digestive biscuits into the tub.
6. Place the lid on the tub and freeze for 24 hours.
7. Remove the tub from the freezer and remove the lid.
8. Use the Quick Start Guide for assembly and processing instructions.
9. Select ICE CREAM program on the Ninja CREAMi.
10. Once processing is complete, scoop the Blueberry Cheesecake ice cream into serving bowls and enjoy immediately.

CHAPTER 01: ICE CREAM

Chocolate Hazelnut Ice Cream

 Serves: 4 ; Prep: 10 Min

Ingredient

- 150ml double cream
- 150ml whole milk
- 50g Nutella (chocolate hazelnut spread)
- 50g caster sugar
- 30g chopped hazelnuts

Per Serving:

Calories: 220; Fat: 15g;
Carbohydrates: 20g; Protein: 2g

Instruction:

1. In a bowl, whisk together the double cream, whole milk, Nutella, and caster sugar until well combined.
2. Pour the mixture into the Ninja CREAMi tub.
3. Sprinkle the chopped hazelnuts into the tub.
4. Place the lid on the tub and freeze for 24 hours.
5. Remove the tub from the freezer and remove the lid.
6. Use the Quick Start Guide for assembly and processing instructions.
7. Select the ICE CREAM program on the Ninja CREAMi.
8. Once processing is complete, scoop the Chocolate Hazelnut ice cream into serving bowls and enjoy immediately.

Lemon Sorbet Ice Cream

 Serves: 4 ; Prep: 10 Min

Ingredient

- 150ml water
- 150g caster sugar
- Zest and juice of 2 lemons

Per Serving:

Calories: 120; Fat: 0g; Carbohydrates: 31g; Protein: 0g

Instruction:

1. In a saucepan, combine the water and caster sugar. Heat over medium heat, stirring occasionally, until the sugar has completely dissolved.
2. Remove the saucepan from the heat and stir in the lemon zest and juice.
3. Allow the mixture to cool to room temperature, then transfer it to a container and refrigerate until chilled.
4. Once chilled, pour the lemon mixture into the Ninja CREAMi tub.
5. Place the lid on the tub and freeze for 24 hours.
6. Remove the tub from the freezer and remove the lid.
7. Follow the Quick Start Guide for assembly and processing instructions.
8. Select the ICE CREAM program on the Ninja CREAMi.
9. Once processing is complete, scoop the Lemon Sorbet ice cream into serving bowls and enjoy immediately.

CHAPTER 01: ICE CREAM

Raspberry Ripple Ice Cream

 Serves: 4 ; Prep: 15 Min

Ingredient

- 150g fresh raspberries
- 50g caster sugar
- 1 tablespoon lemon juice
- 150ml double cream
- 230ml whole milk

Per Serving:

Calories: 180; Fat: 12g; Carbohydrates: 16g; Protein: 2g

Instruction:

1. In a saucepan, combine the raspberries, caster sugar, and lemon juice.
2. Cook over medium heat, stirring occasionally, until the raspberries break down and the sugar dissolves, about 5-7 minutes.
3. Remove from heat and strain the raspberry mixture through a fine mesh sieve to remove the seeds. Allow the raspberry sauce to cool completely.
4. In a separate bowl, whisk together the double cream and whole milk until well combined.
5. Pour the cream mixture into the Ninja CREAMi tub.
6. Drizzle the cooled raspberry sauce over the cream mixture in the tub.
7. Use a spoon to gently swirl the raspberry sauce into the cream mixture to create a ripple effect.
8. Place the lid on the tub and freeze for 24 hours.
9. Remove the tub from the freezer and remove the lid.
10. Follow the Quick Start Guide for assembly and processing instructions.
11. Select the ICE CREAM program on the Ninja CREAMi.
12. Once processing is complete, scoop the Raspberry Ripple ice cream into serving bowls and enjoy immediately.

Mocha Almond Fudge Ice Cream

 Serves: 4 ; Prep: 10 Min

Ingredient

- 150ml double cream
- 230ml whole milk
- 40g caster sugar
- 15g cocoa powder
- 2 teaspoons instant coffee powder
- 50g dark chocolate, chopped
- 30g almonds, chopped

Per Serving:

Calories: 220; Fat: 15g;
Carbohydrates: 18g; Protein: 4g

 Instruction:

1. In a microwave-safe bowl, combine the double cream, whole milk, caster sugar, cocoa powder, and instant coffee powder.
2. Microwave the mixture for 30 seconds, then whisk until the sugar and cocoa powder are fully dissolved.
3. Stir in the chopped dark chocolate until melted and well combined.
4. Pour the mixture into the Ninja CREAMi tub.
5. Sprinkle the chopped almonds over the top of the mixture.
6. Place the lid on the tub and freeze for 24 hours.
7. Remove the tub from the freezer and remove the lid.
8. Follow the Quick Start Guide for assembly and processing instructions.
9. Select the ICE CREAM program on the Ninja CREAMi.
10. Once processing is complete, scoop the Mocha Almond Fudge ice cream into serving bowls and enjoy immediately.

CHAPTER 01: ICE CREAM

Maple Walnut Ice Cream

 Serves: 4 ; Prep: 5 Min

Ingredient

- 150ml double cream
- 230ml whole milk
- 60g maple syrup
- 30g chopped walnuts

Instruction:

1. In a mixing bowl, combine the double cream, whole milk, and maple syrup. Stir until well mixed.
2. Pour the mixture into the Ninja CREAMi tub.
3. Sprinkle the chopped walnuts evenly over the mixture.
4. Place the lid on the tub and freeze for 24 hours.
5. Remove the tub from the freezer and remove the lid.
6. Follow the Quick Start Guide for assembly and processing instructions.
7. Select the ICE CREAM program on the Ninja CREAMi.
8. Once processing is complete, scoop the Maple Walnut ice cream into serving bowls and enjoy immediately.

Per Serving:

Calories: 180; Fat: 14g;
Carbohydrates: 12g; Protein: 3g

Red Velvet Ice Cream

 Serves: 4 ; Prep: 10 Min

Ingredient

- 150ml double cream
- 230ml whole milk
- 50g cream cheese, softened
- 40g caster sugar
- 1 tablespoon cocoa powder
- 1 teaspoon vanilla extract
- Red food coloring (as desired)

Per Serving:

Calories: 180; Fat: 13g;
Carbohydrates: 12g; Protein: 3g

Instruction:

1. In a large mixing bowl, combine the softened cream cheese, caster sugar, cocoa powder, vanilla extract, and red food coloring. Mix until smooth and well combined.
2. Gradually pour in the double cream and whole milk while continuing to mix until the mixture is smooth and homogeneous.
3. Pour the base into the Ninja CREAMi tub.
4. Place the lid on the tub and freeze for 24 hours.
5. Remove the tub from the freezer and remove the lid.
6. Follow the Quick Start Guide for assembly and processing instructions.
7. Select the ICE CREAM program on the Ninja CREAMi.
8. Once processing is complete, scoop the Red Velvet ice cream into serving bowls and enjoy immediately.

CHAPTER 01: ICE CREAM

Banana Nut Ice Cream

 Serves: 4 ; Prep: 10 Min

Ingredient

- 2 ripe bananas, peeled and sliced
- 250ml double cream
- 250ml whole milk
- 50g chopped walnuts
- 50g caster sugar
- 1 teaspoon vanilla extract

Per Serving:

Calories: 320; Fat: 25g;
Carbohydrates: 22g; Protein: 5g

Instruction:

1. In a blender, combine the sliced bananas, double cream, whole milk, caster sugar, and vanilla extract. Blend until smooth.
2. Pour the mixture into the Ninja CREAMi tub.
3. Add the chopped walnuts to the mixture in the tub and stir gently to distribute evenly.
4. Place the lid on the tub and freeze for 24 hours.
5. Remove the tub from the freezer and remove the lid.
6. Follow the Quick Start Guide for assembly and processing instructions.
7. Select the ICE CREAM program on the Ninja CREAMi.
8. Once processing is complete, scoop the Banana Nut ice cream into serving bowls and enjoy immediately.

Key Lime Pie Ice Cream

 Serves: 4 ; Prep: 15 Min

Ingredient

- 4 limes (for zest and juice)
- 250ml double cream
- 250ml whole milk
- 100g caster sugar
- 1 teaspoon vanilla extract
- 100g crushed graham crackers or digestive biscuits

 **Instruction:**

1. Zest and juice the limes. Set aside.
2. In a mixing bowl, whisk together the double cream, whole milk, caster sugar, lime zest, lime juice, and vanilla extract until well combined.
3. Pour the mixture into the Ninja CREAMi tub.
4. Add the crushed graham crackers or digestive biscuits to the mixture in the tub and stir gently to distribute evenly.
5. Place the lid on the tub and freeze for 24 hours.
6. Remove the tub from the freezer and remove the lid.
7. Follow the Quick Start Guide for assembly and processing instructions.
8. Select the ICE CREAM program on the Ninja CREAMi.
9. Once processing is complete, scoop the Key Lime Pie ice cream into serving bowls and enjoy immediately.

Per Serving:

Calories: 320; Fat: 20g;
Carbohydrates: 35g; Protein: 3g

CHAPTER 01: ICE CREAM

Orange Creamsicle Ice Cream

 Serves: 4 ; Prep: 15 Min

Ingredient

- Zest of 2 oranges
- 150ml freshly squeezed orange juice
- 250ml double cream
- 250ml whole milk
- 100g caster sugar
- 1 teaspoon vanilla extract

Instruction:

1. In a mixing bowl, combine the orange zest, freshly squeezed orange juice, double cream, whole milk, caster sugar, and vanilla extract. Stir until the sugar is dissolved.
2. Pour the mixture into the Ninja CREAMi tub.
3. Place the lid on the tub and freeze for 24 hours.
4. Remove the tub from the freezer and remove the lid.
5. Follow the Quick Start Guide for assembly and processing instructions.
6. Select the ICE CREAM program on the Ninja CREAMi.
7. Once processing is complete, scoop the Orange Creamsicle ice cream into serving bowls and enjoy immediately.

Per Serving:

Calories: 280; Fat: 18g;
Carbohydrates: 26g; Protein: 3g

Peppermint Stick Ice Cream

 Serves: 4 ; Prep: 10 Min

Ingredient

- 300ml double cream
- 300ml whole milk
- 100g caster sugar
- 1 teaspoon peppermint extract
- 100g peppermint candies, crushed

 Instruction:

1. In a large mixing bowl, combine the double cream, whole milk, caster sugar, and peppermint extract. Stir until the sugar is dissolved.
2. Pour the mixture into the Ninja CREAMi tub.
3. Add the crushed peppermint candies into the mixture and stir to distribute evenly.
4. Place the lid on the tub and freeze for 24 hours.
5. Remove the tub from the freezer and remove the lid.
6. Follow the Quick Start Guide for assembly and processing instructions.
7. Select the ICE CREAM program on the Ninja CREAMi.
8. Once processing is complete, scoop the Peppermint Stick ice cream into serving bowls and enjoy immediately.

Per Serving:

Calories: 340; Fat: 24g;
Carbohydrates: 30g; Protein: 3g

CHAPTER 01: ICE CREAM

Almond Joy Ice Cream

 Serves: 4 ; Prep: 10 Min

Ingredient

- 200ml double cream
- 200ml whole milk
- 50g caster sugar
- 50g shredded coconut
- 50g chopped almonds
- 50g chocolate chips
- 1 teaspoon almond extract

Instruction:

1. In a large mixing bowl, combine the double cream, whole milk, caster sugar, and almond extract. Stir until the sugar is dissolved.
2. Pour the mixture into the Ninja CREAMi tub.
3. Add the shredded coconut, chopped almonds, and chocolate chips into the mixture and stir to distribute evenly.
4. Place the lid on the tub and freeze for 24 hours.
5. Remove the tub from the freezer and remove the lid.
6. Follow the Quick Start Guide for assembly and processing instructions.
7. Select the ICE CREAM program on the Ninja CREAMi.
8. Once processing is complete, scoop the Almond Joy ice cream into serving bowls and enjoy immediately.

Per Serving:

Calories: 320; Fat: 22g;
Carbohydrates: 28g; Protein: 4g

Honey Lavender Ice Cream

 Serves: 4 ; Prep: 15 Min

Ingredient

- 200ml double cream
- 200ml whole milk
- 50g caster sugar
- 2 tablespoons honey
- 2 tablespoons dried lavender buds

Instruction:

1. In a saucepan, heat the double cream and whole milk over medium heat until it begins to simmer.
2. Stir in the caster sugar until dissolved.
3. Remove from heat and add the honey and dried lavender buds. Let it steep for about 10 minutes.
4. Strain the mixture to remove the lavender buds.
5. Pour the base into the Ninja CREAMi tub.
6. Place the lid on the tub and freeze for 24 hours.
7. Remove the tub from the freezer and remove the lid.
8. Follow the Quick Start Guide for assembly and processing instructions.
9. Select the ICE CREAM program on the Ninja CREAMi.
10. Once processing is complete, scoop the Honey Lavender ice cream into serving bowls and enjoy immediately.

Per Serving:

Calories: 260; Fat: 18g;
Carbohydrates: 22g; Protein: 2g

CHAPTER 01: ICE CREAM

Blueberry Lemonade

 Serves: 4 ; Prep: 15 Min

Ingredient

- 200g fresh blueberries
- 100ml lemon juice
- Zest of 1 lemon
- 150g caster sugar
- 250ml double cream
- 250ml whole milk

Instruction:

1. In a saucepan, combine the fresh blueberries, lemon juice, lemon zest, and caster sugar. Heat over medium heat, stirring occasionally, until the blueberries soften and release their juices. Simmer for 5 minutes, then remove from heat and let cool.
2. Once the blueberry mixture has cooled, blend it until smooth using a blender or food processor.
3. In a large bowl, mix together the blended blueberry mixture, double cream, and whole milk until well combined.
4. Pour the base into the Ninja CREAMi tub.
5. Place the lid on the tub and freeze for 24 hours.
6. Remove the tub from the freezer and remove the lid.
7. Follow the Quick Start Guide for assembly and processing instructions.
8. Select the ICE CREAM program on the Ninja CREAMi.
9. Once processing is complete, scoop the Blueberry Lemonade ice cream into serving bowls and enjoy immediately.

Per Serving:

Calories: 280; Fat: 18g;
Carbohydrates: 28g; Protein: 2g

S'mores Ice Cream

 Serves: 4 ; Prep: 10 Min

Ingredient

- 100g milk chocolate, chopped
- 50g mini marshmallows
- 50g crushed graham crackers
- 150ml double cream
- 250ml whole milk
- 50g caster sugar

 **Instruction:**

1. In a microwave-safe bowl, melt the milk chocolate in 30-second intervals until smooth. Let it cool slightly.
2. In a separate bowl, whisk together the double cream, whole milk, and caster sugar until the sugar is dissolved.
3. Slowly pour the melted chocolate into the cream mixture while whisking continuously until well combined.
4. Pour the base into the Ninja CREAMi tub.
5. Add the mini marshmallows and crushed graham crackers into the mixture in the tub.
6. Place the lid on the tub and freeze for 24 hours.
7. Remove the tub from the freezer and remove the lid.
8. Follow the Quick Start Guide for assembly and processing instructions.
9. Select the ICE CREAM program on the Ninja CREAMi.
10. Once processing is complete, scoop the S'mores ice cream into serving bowls and enjoy immediately.

<u>Per Serving:</u>

Calories: 320; Fat: 20g;
Carbohydrates: 30g; Protein: 5g

CHAPTER 01: ICE CREAM

Cotton Candy Ice Cream

 Serves: 4 ; Prep: 5 Min

Ingredient

- 100g cotton candy (sugar floss), divided into small pieces
- 150ml double cream
- 250ml whole milk
- 50g caster sugar
- A few drops of pink food coloring (optional)

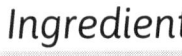 **Instruction:**

1. In a bowl, combine the double cream, whole milk, and caster sugar. Stir until the sugar is dissolved.
2. If using, add a few drops of pink food coloring to the mixture and stir until evenly distributed.
3. Add half of the cotton candy pieces into the cream mixture and stir gently.
4. Pour the mixture into the Ninja CREAMi tub.
5. Sprinkle the remaining cotton candy pieces on top of the mixture in the tub.
6. Place the lid on the tub and freeze for 24 hours.
7. After 24 hours, remove the tub from the freezer and remove the lid.
8. Follow the Quick Start Guide for assembly and processing instructions.
9. Select the ICE CREAM program on the Ninja CREAMi.
10. Once processing is complete, scoop the Cotton Candy ice cream into serving bowls and enjoy immediately.

<u>Per Serving:</u>

Calories: 180; Fat: 12g;
Carbohydrates: 18g; Protein: 2g

Chocolate Coconut Ice Cream

 Serves: 4 ; Prep: 5   Min

- 150g desiccated coconut
- 20g cocoa powder
- 100g caster sugar
- 1 teaspoon vanilla extract
- 150ml double cream
- 250ml whole milk

 ## Instruction:

1. In a large mixing bowl, combine the desiccated coconut, cocoa powder, caster sugar, and vanilla extract.
2. Slowly add the double cream and whole milk to the mixture while stirring continuously until well combined.
3. Pour the mixture into the Ninja CREAMi tub.
4. Place the lid on the tub and freeze for 24 hours.
5. After 24 hours, remove the tub from the freezer and remove the lid.
6. Follow the Quick Start Guide for assembly and processing instructions.
7. Select the ICE CREAM program on the Ninja CREAMi.
8. Once processing is complete, scoop the Chocolate Coconut ice cream into serving bowls and enjoy immediately.

Per Serving:

Calories: 320; Fat: 24g;
Carbohydrates: 26g; Protein: 4g

CHAPTER 01: ICE CREAM

Peanut Butter Banana Ice Cream

 Serves: 4 ; Prep: 5   Min

- 2 ripe bananas, sliced
- 60g smooth peanut butter
- 50g caster sugar
- 150ml double cream
- 250ml whole milk

Instruction:

1. In a blender or food processor, combine the sliced bananas, smooth peanut butter, caster sugar, double cream, and whole milk.
2. Blend the mixture until smooth and creamy.
3. Pour the base into an empty tub of the Ninja CREAMi.
4. Place the lid on the tub and freeze for 24 hours.
5. After 24 hours, remove the tub from the freezer and remove the lid.
6. Follow the Quick Start Guide for assembly and processing instructions.
7. Select the ICE CREAM program on the Ninja CREAMi.
8. Once processing is complete, scoop the Peanut Butter Banana ice cream into serving bowls and enjoy immediately.

Per Serving:

Calories: 280; Fat: 18g;
Carbohydrates: 26g; Protein: 6g

Black Forest Ice Cream

 Serves: 4 ; Prep: 10 Min

Ingredient

- 200g pitted cherries, chopped
- 50g dark chocolate, chopped
- 50g caster sugar
- 150ml double cream
- 250ml whole milk

Instruction:

1. In a saucepan, combine the chopped cherries, chopped dark chocolate, caster sugar, double cream, and whole milk.
2. Heat the mixture over medium heat, stirring continuously until the sugar is dissolved and the chocolate is melted. Do not boil.
3. Remove from heat and let the mixture cool completely.
4. Pour the cooled mixture into the Ninja CREAMi.
5. Place the lid on the tub and freeze for 24 hours.
6. After 24 hours, remove the tub from the freezer and remove the lid.
7. Follow the Quick Start Guide for assembly and processing instructions.
8. Select the ICE CREAM program on the Ninja CREAMi.
9. Once processing is complete, scoop the Black Forest ice cream into serving bowls and enjoy immediately.

Per Serving:

Calories: 220; Fat: 14g; Carbohydrates: 20g; Protein: 3g

CHAPTER 01: ICE CREAM

White Chocolate Raspberry Ice Cream

 Serves: 4 ; Prep: 10 Min

Ingredient

- 100g white chocolate, chopped
- 200g fresh raspberries
- 50g caster sugar
- 150ml double cream
- 250ml whole milk

Instruction:

1. In a saucepan, combine the chopped white chocolate, fresh raspberries, caster sugar, double cream, and whole milk.
2. Heat the mixture over medium heat, stirring continuously until the white chocolate is melted and the sugar is dissolved. Do not boil.
3. Remove from heat and let the mixture cool completely.
4. Pour the cooled mixture into the Ninja CREAMi.
5. Place the lid on the tub and freeze for 24 hours.
6. After 24 hours, remove the tub from the freezer and remove the lid.
7. Follow the Quick Start Guide for assembly and processing instructions.
8. Select the ICE CREAM program on the Ninja CREAMi.
9. Once processing is complete, scoop the White Chocolate Raspberry ice cream into serving bowls and enjoy immediately.

Per Serving:

Calories: 240; Fat: 16g; Carbohydrates: 22g; Protein: 3g

Cinnamon Roll Ice Cream

 Serves: 4 ; Prep: 15 Min

Ingredient

- 2 cinnamon rolls
- 200ml double cream
- 300ml whole milk
- 50g brown sugar
- 1 teaspoon ground cinnamon

 **Instruction:**

1. Cut the cinnamon rolls into small pieces.
2. In a saucepan, combine the double cream, whole milk, brown sugar, and ground cinnamon. Heat the mixture over medium heat, stirring occasionally until the sugar is dissolved. Remove from heat and let it cool.
3. Pour the cooled mixture into the Ninja CREAMi.
4. Add the cinnamon roll pieces into the mixture.
5. Place the lid on the tub and freeze for 24 hours.
6. After 24 hours, remove the tub from the freezer and remove the lid.
7. Follow the Quick Start Guide for assembly and processing instructions.
8. Select the ICE CREAM program on the Ninja CREAMi.
9. Once processing is complete, scoop the Cinnamon Roll ice cream into serving bowls and enjoy immediately.

Per Serving:

Calories: 320; Fat: 20g;
Carbohydrates: 30g; Protein: 5g

CHAPTER 01: ICE CREAM

Mango Tango Ice Cream

 Serves: 4 ; Prep: 10 Min

Ingredient

- 2 ripe mangoes, peeled and diced
- 200ml double cream
- 300ml whole milk
- 50g caster sugar
- 1 teaspoon vanilla extract

Instruction:

1. In a blender, combine the diced mangoes, double cream, whole milk, caster sugar, and vanilla extract. Blend until smooth.
2. Pour the mango mixture into the Ninja CREAMi.
3. Place the lid on the tub and freeze for 24 hours.
4. After 24 hours, remove the tub from the freezer and remove the lid.
5. Follow the Quick Start Guide for assembly and processing instructions.
6. Select the ICE CREAM program on the Ninja CREAMi.
7. Once processing is complete, scoop the Mango Tango ice cream into serving bowls and enjoy immediately.

Per Serving:

Calories: 180; Fat: 10g;
Carbohydrates: 20g; Protein: 2g

Strawberry Shortcake Light Ice Cream

 Serves: 4 ; Prep: 10 Min

 Ingredient

- 225ml double cream
- 140ml semi-skimmed milk
- 1 teaspoon vanilla extract
- 2 tablespoons stevia granules
- 2 tablespoons light agave syrup
- 150g fresh strawberries, chopped

Per Serving:

Calories: 120; Fat: 8g;
Carbohydrates: 10g; Protein: 2g

 Instruction:

1. In a large bowl, combine the double cream, semi-skimmed milk, vanilla extract, stevia granules, and light agave syrup. Whisk until well combined.
2. Add the chopped strawberries to the mixture and stir gently to incorporate.
3. Pour the base into an empty tub. Place the lid on the tub and freeze for 24 hours.
4. After 24 hours, remove the tub from the freezer and remove the lid.
5. Follow the quick instructions for assembly and processing provided in the Ninja CREAMi manual.
6. Select the "LIGHT ICE CREAM" program on the Ninja CREAMi.
7. Once processing is complete, add any desired mix-ins or serve the Strawberry Shortcake Light Ice Cream immediately.

CHAPTER 02: LIGHT ICE CREAM

Mint Chocolate Chip Light Ice Cream

 Serves: 4 ; Prep: 10 Min

Ingredient

- 225ml double cream
- 140ml semi-skimmed milk
- 1 teaspoon peppermint extract
- 2 tablespoons stevia granules
- 2 tablespoons light agave syrup
- 50g dark chocolate, chopped into small chunks

Per Serving:

Calories: 130; Fat: 9g;
Carbohydrates: 11g; Protein: 2g

Instruction:

1. In a large bowl, combine the double cream, semi-skimmed milk, peppermint extract, stevia granules, and light agave syrup. Whisk until well combined.
2. Add the chopped dark chocolate to the mixture and stir gently to incorporate.
3. Pour the base into an empty tub. Place the lid on the tub and freeze for 24 hours.
4. After 24 hours, remove the tub from the freezer and remove the lid.
5. Follow the quick instructions for assembly and processing provided in the Ninja CREAMi manual.
6. Select the "LIGHT ICE CREAM" program on the Ninja CREAMi.
7. Once processing is complete, add any desired mix-ins or serve the Mint Chocolate Chip Light Ice Cream immediately.

Cookies and Cream Light Ice Cream

 Serves: 4 ; Prep: 10 Min

 Ingredient

- 225ml double cream
- 140ml semi-skimmed milk
- 2 tablespoons stevia granules
- 2 tablespoons light agave syrup
- 100g chocolate sandwich cookies, crushed into small pieces

Per Serving:

Calories: 180; Fat: 12g;
Carbohydrates: 16g; Protein: 2g

 Instruction:

1. In a large bowl, combine the double cream, semi-skimmed milk, stevia granules, and light agave syrup. Whisk until well combined.
2. Add the crushed chocolate sandwich cookies to the mixture and stir gently to incorporate.
3. Pour the base into an empty tub. Place the lid on the tub and freeze for 24 hours.
4. After 24 hours, remove the tub from the freezer and remove the lid.
5. Follow the quick instructions for assembly and processing provided in the Ninja CREAMi manual.
6. Select the "LIGHT ICE CREAM" program on the Ninja CREAMi.
7. Once processing is complete, add any desired mix-ins or serve the Cookies and Cream Light Ice Cream immediately.

CHAPTER 02: LIGHT ICE CREAM

Coffee Toffee Light Ice Cream

 Serves: 6 ; Prep: 15 Min

Ingredient

- 225ml double cream
- 140ml semi-skimmed milk
- 2 tablespoons stevia granules
- 2 tablespoons light agave syrup
- 2 tablespoons instant coffee granules
- 50g toffee pieces

Per Serving:

Calories: 160; Fat: 10g;
Carbohydrates: 15g; Protein: 2g

Instruction:

1. In a large bowl, combine the double cream, semi-skimmed milk, stevia granules, light agave syrup, and instant coffee granules. Whisk until well combined.
2. Add the toffee pieces to the mixture and stir gently to incorporate.
3. Pour the base into an empty tub. Place the lid on the tub and freeze for 24 hours.
4. After 24 hours, remove the tub from the freezer and remove the lid.
5. Follow the quick instructions for assembly and processing provided in the Ninja CREAMi manual.
6. Select the "LIGHT ICE CREAM" program on the Ninja CREAMi.
7. Once processing is complete, add any desired mix-ins or serve the Coffee Toffee Light Ice Cream immediately.

Peanut Butter Swirl Light Ice Cream

 Serves: 6 ; Prep: 10 Min

Ingredient

- 300ml semi-skimmed milk
- 200ml double cream
- 60g peanut butter
- 3 tablespoons light agave syrup
- 2 tablespoons stevia granules

Per Serving:

Calories: 120; Fat: 9g;
Carbohydrates: 7g; Protein: 3g

Instruction:

1. In a large bowl, whisk together semi-skimmed milk, double cream, light agave syrup, and stevia granules until well combined.
2. Pour the base into an empty tub. Place the lid on the tub and freeze for 24 hours.
3. Remove the tub from the freezer and remove the lid.
4. Select the "LIGHT ICE CREAM" program on your Ninja CREAMi.
5. Once processing is complete, add swirls of peanut butter into the ice cream using a spoon.
6. Serve immediately and enjoy!

CHAPTER 02: LIGHT ICE CREAM

Rocky Road Light Ice Cream

 Serves: 6 ; Prep: 10 Min

Ingredient

- 300ml semi-skimmed milk
- 200ml double cream
- 50g dark chocolate chips
- 50g mini marshmallows
- 30g chopped almonds
- 3 tablespoons light agave syrup
- 2 tablespoons stevia granules

Per Serving:

Calories: 160; Fat: 10g;
Carbohydrates: 13g; Protein: 4g

Instruction:

1. In a large bowl, whisk together semi-skimmed milk, double cream, light agave syrup, and stevia granules until well combined.
2. Pour the base into an empty tub. Place the lid on the tub and freeze for 24 hours.
3. Remove the tub from the freezer and remove the lid.
4. Select the "LIGHT ICE CREAM" program on your Ninja CREAMi.
5. Once processing is complete, add dark chocolate chips, mini marshmallows, and chopped almonds into the ice cream.
6. Serve immediately and enjoy!

Coconut Almond Joy Light Ice Cream

 Serves: 6 ; Prep: 10 Min

 Ingredient

- 280ml semi-skimmed milk
- 200ml double cream
- 40g shredded coconut
- 40g chopped almonds
- 50g dark chocolate chips
- 3 tablespoons light agave syrup
- 2 tablespoons stevia granules

 **Instruction:**

1. In a large bowl, whisk together semi-skimmed milk, double cream, light agave syrup, and stevia granules until well combined.
2. Pour the base into an empty tub. Place the lid on the tub and freeze for 24 hours.
3. Remove the tub from the freezer and remove the lid.
4. Select the "LIGHT ICE CREAM" program on your Ninja CREAMi.
5. Once processing is complete, add shredded coconut, chopped almonds, and dark chocolate chips into the ice cream.
6. Serve immediately and enjoy!

Per Serving:

Calories: 180; Fat: 12g;
Carbohydrates: 13g; Protein: 4g

CHAPTER 02: LIGHT ICE CREAM

Birthday Cake Light Ice Cream

 Serves: 6 ; Prep: 10 Min

 Ingredient

- 280ml semi-skimmed milk
- 200ml double cream
- 50g rainbow sprinkles
- 3 tablespoons light agave syrup
- 2 tablespoons stevia granules
- 1 teaspoon vanilla extract

Instruction:

1. In a large bowl, whisk together semi-skimmed milk, double cream, light agave syrup, stevia granules, and vanilla extract until well combined.
2. Pour the base into an empty tub. Place the lid on the tub and freeze for 24 hours.
3. Remove the tub from the freezer and remove the lid.
4. Select the "LIGHT ICE CREAM" program on your Ninja CREAMi.
5. Once processing is complete, add rainbow sprinkles into the ice cream.
6. Serve immediately and enjoy!

Per Serving:

Calories: 150; Fat: 10g;
Carbohydrates: 14g; Protein: 3g

Pistachio Light Ice Cream

 Serves: 6 ; Prep: 10 Min

Ingredient

- 280ml semi-skimmed milk
- 200ml double cream
- 50g shelled pistachios, finely chopped
- 3 tablespoons light agave syrup
- 2 tablespoons stevia granules
- 1 teaspoon almond extract

Per Serving:

Calories: 160; Fat: 11g;
Carbohydrates: 12g; Protein: 3g

Instruction:

1. In a large bowl, whisk together semi-skimmed milk, double cream, light agave syrup, stevia granules, and almond extract until well combined.
2. Pour the base into an empty tub. Place the lid on the tub and freeze for 24 hours.
3. Remove the tub from the freezer and remove the lid.
4. Select the "LIGHT ICE CREAM" program on your Ninja CREAMi.
5. Once processing is complete, add finely chopped pistachios into the ice cream.
6. Serve immediately and enjoy!

CHAPTER 02: LIGHT ICE CREAM

Neapolitan Light Ice Cream

 Serves: 6 ; Prep: 20 Min

Ingredient

- 280ml semi-skimmed milk
- 200ml double cream
- 3 tablespoons light agave syrup
- 2 tablespoons stevia granules
- 1 teaspoon vanilla extract
- 30g cocoa powder
- 50g strawberries, chopped

Per Serving:

Calories: 140; Fat: 9g;
Carbohydrates: 11g; Protein: 3g

Instruction:

1. In a large bowl, whisk together semi-skimmed milk, double cream, light agave syrup, stevia granules, and vanilla extract until well combined.
2. Divide the base into three equal portions.
3. Pour one portion into an empty tub. Place the lid on the tub and freeze for 24 hours.
4. Remove the tub from the freezer and remove the lid.
5. Add cocoa powder to the second portion of the base and mix until well combined.
6. Pour the chocolate mixture into another empty tub. Place the lid on the tub and freeze for 24 hours.
7. Remove the tub from the freezer and remove the lid.
8. Add chopped strawberries to the third portion of the base and mix until well combined.
9. Pour the strawberry mixture into another empty tub. Place the lid on the tub and freeze for 24 hours.
10. Select the "LIGHT ICE CREAM" program on your Ninja CREAMi.
11. Once processing is complete, remove each tub from the freezer, scoop each flavor into serving bowls, and enjoy the Neapolitan light ice cream!

Salted Caramel Light Ice Cream

 Serves: 6 ; Prep: 10 Min

Ingredient

- 280ml semi-skimmed milk
- 200ml double cream
- 3 tablespoons light agave syrup
- 2 tablespoons stevia granules
- 1 teaspoon vanilla extract
- 50g caramel sauce
- Pinch of sea salt

<u>Per Serving:</u>

Calories: 150; Fat: 10g;
Carbohydrates: 12g; Protein: 3g

Instruction:

1. In a large bowl, whisk together semi-skimmed milk, double cream, light agave syrup, stevia granules, and vanilla extract until well combined.
2. Pour the base into an empty tub. Drizzle caramel sauce over the top and sprinkle with a pinch of sea salt. Use a spoon to gently swirl the caramel and salt into the mixture.
3. Place the lid on the tub and freeze for 24 hours.
4. Remove the tub from the freezer and remove the lid.
5. Select the "LIGHT ICE CREAM" program on your Ninja CREAMi.
6. Once processing is complete, serve immediately and enjoy the creamy and delicious salted caramel light ice cream!

CHAPTER 02: LIGHT ICE CREAM

Chocolate Brownie Light Ice Cream

 Serves: 6 ; Prep: 15 Min

Ingredient

- 280ml semi-skimmed milk
- 200ml double cream
- 3 tablespoons light agave syrup
- 2 tablespoons stevia granules
- 1 teaspoon vanilla extract
- 50g dark chocolate, chopped
- 50g brownie pieces

Instruction:

1. In a large bowl, whisk together semi-skimmed milk, double cream, light agave syrup, stevia granules, and vanilla extract until well combined.
2. Pour the base into an empty tub. Add chopped dark chocolate and brownie pieces into the mixture and stir until evenly distributed.
3. Place the lid on the tub and freeze for 24 hours.
4. Remove the tub from the freezer and remove the lid.
5. Select the "LIGHT ICE CREAM" program on your Ninja CREAMi.
6. Once processing is complete, serve immediately and enjoy the rich and creamy chocolate brownie light ice cream!

<u>Per Serving:</u>

Calories: 170; Fat: 11g;
Carbohydrates: 14g; Protein: 3g

Cherry Vanilla Light Ice Cream

 Serves: 6 ; Prep: 15 Min

 Ingredient

- 280ml semi-skimmed milk
- 200ml double cream
- 3 tablespoons light agave syrup
- 2 tablespoons stevia granules
- 1 teaspoon vanilla extract
- 100g fresh cherries, pitted and chopped

Instruction:

1. In a large bowl, whisk together semi-skimmed milk, double cream, light agave syrup, stevia granules, and vanilla extract until well combined.
2. Pour the base into an empty tub. Add chopped fresh cherries into the mixture and stir until evenly distributed.
3. Place the lid on the tub and freeze for 24 hours.
4. Remove the tub from the freezer and remove the lid.
5. Select the "LIGHT ICE CREAM" program on your Ninja CREAMi.
6. Once processing is complete, serve immediately and enjoy the delightful cherry vanilla light ice cream!

Per Serving:

Calories: 140; Fat: 9g;
Carbohydrates: 12g; Protein: 3g

CHAPTER 02: LIGHT ICE CREAM

Blueberry Cheesecake Light Ice Cream

 Serves: 6 ; Prep: 15 Min

 Ingredient

- 280ml semi-skimmed milk
- 200ml double cream
- 3 tablespoons light agave syrup
- 2 tablespoons stevia granules
- 1 teaspoon vanilla extract
- 100g fresh blueberries
- 50g crushed digestive biscuits

Instruction:

1. In a large bowl, whisk together semi-skimmed milk, double cream, light agave syrup, stevia granules, and vanilla extract until well combined.
2. Pour the base into an empty tub. Add fresh blueberries and crushed digestive biscuits into the mixture and stir until evenly distributed.
3. Place the lid on the tub and freeze for 24 hours.
4. Remove the tub from the freezer and remove the lid.
5. Select the "LIGHT ICE CREAM" program on your Ninja CREAMi.
6. Once processing is complete, serve immediately and enjoy the delicious blueberry cheesecake light ice cream!

Per Serving:

Calories: 160; Fat: 11g;
Carbohydrates: 13g; Protein: 3g

Lemon Sorbet Light Ice Cream

 Serves: 6 ; Prep: 10 Min

Ingredient

- 280ml water
- 200ml double cream
- Juice and zest of 2 lemons
- 4 tablespoons light agave syrup
- 2 tablespoons stevia granules

 **Instruction:**

1. In a large bowl, whisk together water, double cream, lemon juice, lemon zest, light agave syrup, and stevia granules until well combined.
2. Pour the sorbet base into an empty tub.
3. Place the lid on the tub and freeze for 24 hours.
4. Remove the tub from the freezer and remove the lid.
5. Select the "LIGHT ICE CREAM" program on your Ninja CREAMi.
6. Once processing is complete, serve immediately and enjoy the refreshing lemon sorbet light ice cream!

Per Serving:

Calories: 90; Fat: 7g;
Carbohydrates: 6g; Protein: 1g

CHAPTER 02: LIGHT ICE CREAM

Raspberry Swirl Light Ice Cream

 Serves: 6 ; Prep: 15 Min

Ingredient

- 280ml semi-skimmed milk
- 200ml double cream
- 3 tablespoons light agave syrup
- 2 tablespoons stevia granules
- 1 teaspoon vanilla extract
- 100g fresh raspberries
- 2 tablespoons raspberry jam

 Instruction:

1. In a large bowl, whisk together semi-skimmed milk, double cream, light agave syrup, stevia granules, and vanilla extract until well combined.
2. Pour the base into an empty tub.
3. In a separate small bowl, mash the fresh raspberries with a fork until smooth.
4. Swirl the raspberry jam and mashed raspberries into the ice cream mixture using a spoon or spatula.
5. Place the lid on the tub and freeze for 24 hours.
6. Remove the tub from the freezer and remove the lid.
7. Select the "LIGHT ICE CREAM" program on your Ninja CREAMi.
8. Once processing is complete, serve immediately and enjoy the delightful raspberry swirl light ice cream!

Per Serving:

Calories: 150; Fat: 10g;
Carbohydrates: 12g; Protein: 3g

Mocha Almond Fudge Light Ice Cream

 Serves: 6 ; Prep: 15 Min

Ingredient

- 280ml semi-skimmed milk
- 200ml double cream
- 3 tablespoons light agave syrup
- 2 tablespoons stevia granules
- 2 tablespoons cocoa powder
- 1 teaspoon instant coffee granules
- 50g dark chocolate, chopped
- 50g almonds, chopped

Instruction:

1. In a large bowl, whisk together semi-skimmed milk, double cream, light agave syrup, stevia granules, cocoa powder, and instant coffee granules until well combined.
2. Pour the base into an empty tub.
3. Add chopped dark chocolate and almonds into the mixture and stir until evenly distributed.
4. Place the lid on the tub and freeze for 24 hours.
5. Remove the tub from the freezer and remove the lid.
6. Select the "LIGHT ICE CREAM" program on your Ninja CREAMi.
7. Once processing is complete, serve immediately and enjoy the indulgent mocha almond fudge light ice cream!

Per Serving:

Calories: 160; Fat: 11g;
Carbohydrates: 12g; Protein: 3g

CHAPTER 02: LIGHT ICE CREAM

Maple Walnut Light Ice Cream

 Serves: 6 ; Prep: 10 Min

Ingredient

- 280ml semi-skimmed milk
- 200ml double cream
- 3 tablespoons maple syrup
- 2 tablespoons stevia granules
- 1 teaspoon vanilla extract
- 50g walnuts, chopped

Instruction:

1. In a large bowl, whisk together semi-skimmed milk, double cream, maple syrup, stevia granules, and vanilla extract until well combined.
2. Pour the base into an empty tub.
3. Add chopped walnuts into the mixture and stir until evenly distributed.
4. Place the lid on the tub and freeze for 24 hours.
5. Remove the tub from the freezer and remove the lid.
6. Select the "LIGHT ICE CREAM" program on your Ninja CREAMi.
7. Once processing is complete, serve immediately and enjoy the delightful maple walnut light ice cream!

Per Serving:

Calories: 160; Fat: 12g;
Carbohydrates: 9g; Protein: 3g

Peppermint Stick Light Ice Cream

 Serves: 6 ; Prep: 10 Min

Ingredient

- 280ml semi-skimmed milk
- 200ml double cream
- 3 tablespoons light agave syrup
- 2 tablespoons stevia granules
- 1 teaspoon peppermint extract
- 50g dark chocolate, chopped
- 50g peppermint candies, crushed

 **Instruction:**

1. Combine semi-skimmed milk, double cream, light agave syrup, stevia granules, and peppermint extract in a large bowl. Mix well.
2. Pour the mixture into an empty tub.
3. Add chopped dark chocolate and crushed peppermint candies to the mixture. Stir gently to distribute evenly.
4. Place the lid on the tub and freeze for 24 hours.
5. Remove the tub from the freezer and let it sit for a few minutes.
6. Select the "LIGHT ICE CREAM" program on your Ninja CREAMi.
7. Once processing is complete, serve immediately and enjoy the refreshing peppermint stick light ice cream!

Per Serving:

Calories: 190; Fat: 12g;
Carbohydrates: 18g; Protein: 3g

CHAPTER 02: LIGHT ICE CREAM

Orange Creamsicle Light Ice Cream

 Serves: 6 ; Prep: 15 Min

Ingredient

- 280ml semi-skimmed milk
- 200ml double cream
- Zest of 1 orange
- 3 tablespoons light agave syrup
- 2 tablespoons stevia granules
- 1 teaspoon vanilla extract
- 100ml freshly squeezed orange juice

Instruction:

1. In a large bowl, combine semi-skimmed milk, double cream, orange zest, light agave syrup, stevia granules, vanilla extract, and freshly squeezed orange juice. Mix well.
2. Pour the mixture into an empty tub.
3. Place the lid on the tub and freeze for 24 hours.
4. Remove the tub from the freezer and let it sit for a few minutes.
5. Select the "LIGHT ICE CREAM" program on your Ninja CREAMi.
6. Once processing is complete, serve immediately and enjoy the refreshing Orange Creamsicle light ice cream!

Per Serving:

Calories: 160; Fat: 10g;
Carbohydrates: 15g; Protein: 2g

Lemon Sorbet

 Serves: 6 ; Prep: 20 Min

Ingredient

- 4 large lemons
- 200g granulated sugar
- 300ml water

Per Serving:

Calories: 120; Fat: 0g;
Carbohydrates: 31g; Protein: 0g

Instruction:

1. Zest and juice the lemons. Set aside.
2. In a saucepan, combine granulated sugar and water. Heat over medium heat, stirring occasionally, until the sugar has completely dissolved.
3. Remove the sugar syrup from the heat and let it cool to room temperature.
4. Once cooled, add the lemon zest and juice to the sugar syrup. Stir well to combine.
5. Pour the mixture through a fine-mesh sieve into an empty tub. Place the lid on the tub and freeze for 24 hours.
6. Remove the tub from the freezer and let it sit for a few minutes.
7. Select the "SORBET" program on your Ninja CREAMi.
8. Once processing is complete, serve immediately or transfer the sorbet to a container and freeze for firmer texture.

CHAPTER 03: SORBET

Raspberry Sorbet

 Serves: 6 ; Prep: 20 Min

Ingredient

- 500g fresh raspberries
- 150g granulated sugar
- 200ml water

Per Serving:

Calories: 120; Fat: 0g;
Carbohydrates: 30g; Protein: 1g

Instruction:

1. Rinse the raspberries under cold water and pat them dry with paper towels.
2. In a saucepan, combine granulated sugar and water. Heat over medium heat, stirring occasionally, until the sugar has completely dissolved.
3. Remove the sugar syrup from the heat and let it cool to room temperature.
4. In a blender or food processor, blend the raspberries until smooth.
5. Strain the raspberry puree through a fine-mesh sieve into a bowl to remove the seeds.
6. Stir the cooled sugar syrup into the raspberry puree until well combined.
7. Pour the mixture through a fine-mesh sieve into an empty tub. Place the lid on the tub and freeze for 24 hours.
8. Remove the tub from the freezer and let it sit for a few minutes.
9. Select the "SORBET" program on your Ninja CREAMi.
10. Once processing is complete, serve immediately or transfer the sorbet to a container and freeze for firmer texture.

Strawberry Sorbet

Serves: 6 ; Prep: 10 Min

Ingredient

- 500g fresh strawberries, cleaned and sliced
- 100g granulated sugar
- 200ml hot water (60-70°C)

Instruction:

1. In a large bowl, combine the sliced strawberries and granulated sugar. Mash them together using a fork until the sugar is dissolved and the strawberries release their juices.
2. Add the hot water to the strawberry mixture and stir until well combined.
3. Pour the mixture through a fine-mesh sieve into an empty tub. Place the lid on the tub and freeze for 24 hours.
4. Remove the tub from the freezer and let it sit at room temperature for a few minutes.
5. Select the "SORBET" program on your Ninja CREAMi.
6. Once processing is complete, serve the sorbet immediately or transfer it to a container and freeze for a firmer texture.

Per Serving:

Calories: 90; Fat: 0g;
Carbohydrates: 23g; Protein: 1g

CHAPTER 03: SORBET

Mango Sorbet

Serves: 6 ; Prep: 10 Min

Ingredient

- 600g ripe mango, peeled and diced
- 100g granulated sugar
- 200ml hot water (60-70°C)

Instruction:

1. In a blender or food processor, combine the diced mango and granulated sugar. Blend until smooth.
2. Add the hot water to the mango mixture and blend again until well combined.
3. Pour the mixture through a fine-mesh sieve into an empty tub. Place the lid on the tub and freeze for 24 hours.
4. Remove the tub from the freezer and let it sit at room temperature for a few minutes.
5. Select the "SORBET" program on your Ninja CREAMi.
6. Once processing is complete, serve the sorbet immediately or transfer it to a container and freeze for a firmer texture.

Per Serving:

Calories: 120; Fat: 0.5g;
Carbohydrates: 30g; Protein: 1g

Pineapple Sorbet

Serves: 6 ; Prep: 10 Min

Ingredient

- 500g fresh pineapple chunks
- 100g granulated sugar
- 200ml hot water (60-70°C)

Instruction:

1. In a blender or food processor, combine the pineapple chunks and granulated sugar. Blend until smooth.
2. Add the hot water to the pineapple mixture and blend again until well combined.
3. Pour the mixture through a fine-mesh sieve into an empty tub. Place the lid on the tub and freeze for 24 hours.
4. Remove the tub from the freezer and let it sit at room temperature for a few minutes.
5. Select the "SORBET" program on your Ninja CREAMi.
6. Once processing is complete, serve the sorbet immediately or transfer it to a container and freeze for a firmer texture.

Per Serving:

Calories: 100; Fat: 0.1g;
Carbohydrates: 26g; Protein: 0.5g

CHAPTER 03: SORBET

Watermelon Sorbet

Serves: 6 ; Prep: 10 Min

Ingredient

- 800g fresh watermelon chunks
- 100g granulated sugar
- 200ml hot water (60-70°C)

Instruction:

1. In a blender or food processor, combine the watermelon chunks and granulated sugar. Blend until smooth.
2. Add the hot water to the watermelon mixture and blend again until well combined.
3. Pour the mixture through a fine-mesh sieve into an empty tub. Place the lid on the tub and freeze for 24 hours.
4. Remove the tub from the freezer and let it sit at room temperature for a few minutes.
5. Select the "SORBET" program on your Ninja CREAMi.
6. Once processing is complete, serve the sorbet immediately or transfer it to a container and freeze for a firmer texture.

Per Serving:

Calories: 80; Fat: 0.2g;
Carbohydrates: 20g; Protein: 0.6g

Blueberry Sorbet

Serves: 6 ; Prep: 10 Min

Ingredient

- 500g fresh blueberries
- 100g granulated sugar
- 150ml hot water (60-70°C)

Instruction:

1. In a blender or food processor, combine the fresh blueberries and granulated sugar. Blend until smooth.
2. Add the hot water to the blueberry mixture and blend again until well combined.
3. Pour the mixture through a fine-mesh sieve into an empty tub. Place the lid on the tub and freeze for 24 hours.
4. Remove the tub from the freezer and let it sit at room temperature for a few minutes.
5. Select the "SORBET" program on your Ninja CREAMi.
6. Once processing is complete, serve the sorbet immediately or transfer it to a container and freeze for a firmer texture.

Per Serving:

Calories: 100; Fat: 0.2g;
Carbohydrates: 25g; Protein: 1g

CHAPTER 03: SORBET

Peach Sorbet

Serves: 6 ; Prep: 10 Min

Ingredient

- 500g fresh peaches, peeled and diced
- 100g granulated sugar
- 150ml hot water (60-70°C)

Instruction:

1. In a blender or food processor, combine the fresh peaches and granulated sugar. Blend until smooth.
2. Add the hot water to the peach mixture and blend again until well combined.
3. Pour the mixture through a fine-mesh sieve into an empty tub. Place the lid on the tub and freeze for 24 hours.
4. Remove the tub from the freezer and let it sit at room temperature for a few minutes.
5. Select the "SORBET" program on your Ninja CREAMi.
6. Once processing is complete, serve the sorbet immediately or transfer it to a container and freeze for a firmer texture.

Per Serving:

Calories: 110; Fat: 0.2g;
Carbohydrates: 27g; Protein: 1g

Kiwi Sorbet

Serves: 6 ; Prep: 10 Min

Ingredient

- 500g ripe kiwis, peeled and diced
- 100g granulated sugar
- 150ml hot water (60-70°C)

Instruction:

1. In a blender or food processor, combine the ripe kiwis and granulated sugar. Blend until smooth.
2. Add the hot water to the kiwi mixture and blend again until well combined.
3. Pour the mixture through a fine-mesh sieve into an empty tub. Place the lid on the tub and freeze for 24 hours.
4. Remove the tub from the freezer and let it sit at room temperature for a few minutes.
5. Select the "SORBET" program on your Ninja CREAMi.
6. Once processing is complete, serve the sorbet immediately or transfer it to a container and freeze for a firmer texture.

Per Serving:

Calories: 90; Fat: 0.5g;
Carbohydrates: 22g; Protein: 1g

CHAPTER 03: SORBET

Passionfruit Sorbet

Serves: 6 ; Prep: 15 Min

Ingredient

- 10 ripe passionfruits
- 100g granulated sugar
- 150ml hot water (60-70°C)

Instruction:

1. Cut the passionfruits in half and scoop out the pulp into a blender or food processor.
2. Add the granulated sugar to the passionfruit pulp.
3. Blend the mixture until smooth.
4. Pour the hot water into the blender and blend again until well combined.
5. Strain the mixture through a fine-mesh sieve into an empty tub. Place the lid on the tub and freeze for 24 hours.
6. After freezing, remove the tub from the freezer and let it sit at room temperature for a few minutes.
7. Select the "SORBET" program on your Ninja CREAMi.
8. Once processing is complete, serve the sorbet immediately or transfer it to a container and freeze for a firmer texture.

Per Serving:

Calories: 110; Fat: 0.5g;
Carbohydrates: 27g; Protein: 1g

Lime Sorbet

Serves: 6 ; **Prep:** 15 Min

Ingredient

- 4 large limes
- 150g granulated sugar
- 200ml hot water (60-70°C)

Instruction:

1. Zest and juice the limes, then combine the zest, juice, and granulated sugar in a blender or food processor.
2. Blend until the sugar is dissolved and the mixture is smooth.
3. Pour in the hot water and blend again until well combined.
4. Strain the mixture through a fine-mesh sieve into an empty tub. Place the lid on the tub and freeze for 24 hours.
5. After freezing, remove the tub from the freezer and let it sit at room temperature for a few minutes.
6. Select the "SORBET" program on your Ninja CREAMi.
7. Once processing is complete, serve the sorbet immediately or transfer it to a container and freeze for a firmer texture.

Per Serving:

Calories: 120; Fat: 0g;
Carbohydrates: 31g; Protein: 0.5g

CHAPTER 03: SORBET

Orange Sorbet

Serves: 6 ; **Prep:** 15 Min

Ingredient

- 4 large oranges
- 150g granulated sugar
- 200ml hot water (60-70°C)

Instruction:

1. Zest and juice the oranges, then combine the zest, juice, and granulated sugar in a blender or food processor.
2. Blend until the sugar is dissolved and the mixture is smooth.
3. Pour in the hot water and blend again until well combined.
4. Strain the mixture through a fine-mesh sieve into an empty tub. Place the lid on the tub and freeze for 24 hours.
5. After freezing, remove the tub from the freezer and let it sit at room temperature for a few minutes.
6. Select the "SORBET" program on your Ninja CREAMi.
7. Once processing is complete, serve the sorbet immediately or transfer it to a container and freeze for a firmer texture.

Per Serving:

Calories: 110; Fat: 0g;
Carbohydrates: 28g; Protein: 0.5g

Grapefruit Sorbet

Serves: 6 ; Prep: 15 Min

Ingredient

- 3 large grapefruits
- 100g granulated sugar
- 150ml hot water (60-70°C)

Instruction:

1. Juice the grapefruits and strain the juice to remove any pulp or seeds.
2. In a blender or food processor, combine the grapefruit juice and granulated sugar. Blend until the sugar is dissolved.
3. Pour in the hot water and blend again until well combined.
4. Strain the mixture through a fine-mesh sieve into an empty tub. Place the lid on the tub and freeze for 24 hours.
5. After freezing, remove the tub from the freezer and let it sit at room temperature for a few minutes.
6. Select the "SORBET" program on your Ninja CREAMi.
7. Once processing is complete, serve the sorbet immediately or transfer it to a container and freeze for a firmer texture.

Per Serving:

Calories: 90; Fat: 0g;
Carbohydrates: 23g; Protein: 0.5g

CHAPTER 03: SORBET

Coconut Sorbet

Serves: 6 ; Prep: 5 Min

Ingredient

- 400ml coconut milk
- 100g granulated sugar
- 75ml hot water (60-70°C)

Instruction:

1. In a mixing bowl, combine the coconut milk and granulated sugar. Stir until the sugar is completely dissolved.
2. Add the hot water to the mixture and stir until well combined.
3. Pour the mixture through a fine-mesh sieve into an empty tub. Place the lid on the tub and freeze for 24 hours.
4. After freezing, remove the tub from the freezer and let it sit at room temperature for a few minutes.
5. Select the "SORBET" program on your Ninja CREAMi.
6. Once processing is complete, serve the sorbet immediately or transfer it to a container and freeze for a firmer texture.

Per Serving:

Calories: 180; Fat: 12g;
Carbohydrates: 18g; Protein: 1g

Blackberry Sorbet

Serves: 6 ; Prep: 10 Min

Ingredient

- 500g fresh blackberries
- 100g granulated sugar
- 75ml hot water (60-70°C)

Instruction:

1. In a large bowl, add the blackberries and granulated sugar. Mash them with a fork until well combined and juicy.
2. Pour the hot water over the blackberry mixture and stir until the sugar is completely dissolved.
3. Pass the mixture through a fine-mesh sieve into an empty tub. Place the lid on the tub and freeze for 24 hours.
4. Remove the tub from the freezer and let it sit at room temperature for a few minutes.
5. Select the "SORBET" program on your Ninja CREAMi.
6. Once processing is complete, serve the sorbet immediately or transfer it to a container and freeze for a firmer texture.

Per Serving:

Calories: 100; Fat: 0.5g;
Carbohydrates: 24g; Protein: 1g

CHAPTER 03: SORBET

Cranberry Sorbet

Serves: 6 ; Prep: 10 Min

Ingredient

- 500g fresh cranberries
- 100g granulated sugar
- 75ml hot water (60-70°C)

Instruction:

1. In a large bowl, combine the cranberries and granulated sugar. Mash them together until the cranberries release their juices and the sugar is dissolved.
2. Add the hot water to the cranberry mixture and stir until well combined.
3. Pour the mixture through a fine-mesh sieve into an empty tub. Place the lid on the tub and freeze for 24 hours.
4. Remove the tub from the freezer and let it sit at room temperature for a few minutes.
5. Select the "SORBET" program on your Ninja CREAMi.
6. Once processing is complete, serve the sorbet immediately or transfer it to a container and freeze for a firmer texture.

Per Serving:

Calories: 120; Fat: 0.2g;
Carbohydrates: 31g; Protein: 0.5g

Cherry Sorbet

Serves: 6 ; Prep: 10 Min

Ingredient

- 500g fresh cherries, pitted
- 100g granulated sugar
- 75ml hot water (60-70°C)

Instruction:

1. In a large bowl, combine the pitted cherries and granulated sugar. Mash them together until the cherries release their juices and the sugar is dissolved.
2. Add the hot water to the cherry mixture and stir until well combined.
3. Pour the mixture through a fine-mesh sieve into an empty tub. Place the lid on the tub and freeze for 24 hours.
4. Remove the tub from the freezer and let it sit at room temperature for a few minutes.
5. Select the "SORBET" program on your Ninja CREAMi.
6. Once processing is complete, serve the sorbet immediately or transfer it to a container and freeze for a firmer texture.

Per Serving:

Calories: 120; Fat: 0.3g;
Carbohydrates: 30g; Protein: 0.9g

CHAPTER 03: SORBET

Green Apple Sorbet

Serves: 6 ; Prep: 10 Min

Ingredient

- 500g green apples, peeled, cored, and chopped
- 100g granulated sugar
- 75ml hot water (60-70°C)

Instruction:

1. In a blender or food processor, combine the chopped green apples and granulated sugar. Blend until smooth.
2. Add the hot water to the apple mixture and blend again until well combined.
3. Pour the mixture through a fine-mesh sieve into an empty tub. Place the lid on the tub and freeze for 24 hours.
4. Remove the tub from the freezer and let it sit at room temperature for a few minutes.
5. Select the "SORBET" program on your Ninja CREAMi.
6. Once processing is complete, serve the sorbet immediately or transfer it to a container and freeze for a firmer texture.

Per Serving:

Calories: 110; Fat: 0.1g;
Carbohydrates: 28g; Protein: 0.4g

Pear Sorbet

Serves: 6 ; Prep: 10 Min

Ingredient

- 500g ripe pears, peeled, cored, and chopped
- 100g granulated sugar
- 75ml hot water (60-70°C)

Instruction:

1. In a blender or food processor, combine the chopped pears and granulated sugar. Blend until smooth.
2. Add the hot water to the pear mixture and blend again until well combined.
3. Pour the mixture through a fine-mesh sieve into an empty tub. Place the lid on the tub and freeze for 24 hours.
4. Remove the tub from the freezer and let it sit at room temperature for a few minutes.
5. Select the "SORBET" program on your Ninja CREAMi.
6. Once processing is complete, serve the sorbet immediately or transfer it to a container and freeze for a firmer texture.

Per Serving:

Calories: 110; Fat: 0.1g;
Carbohydrates: 28g; Protein: 0.4g

CHAPTER 03: SORBET

Papaya Sorbet

Serves: 6 ; Prep: 10 Min

Ingredient

- 500g ripe papaya, peeled, seeded, and diced
- 100g caster sugar
- 75ml hot water (60-70°C)

Instruction:

1. In a blender or food processor, combine the diced papaya and caster sugar. Blend until smooth.
2. Add the hot water to the papaya mixture and blend again until well combined.
3. Pour the mixture through a fine-mesh sieve into an empty tub. Place the lid on the tub and freeze for 24 hours.
4. Remove the tub from the freezer and let it sit at room temperature for a few minutes.
5. Select the "SORBET" program on your Ninja CREAMi.
6. Once processing is complete, serve the sorbet immediately or transfer it to a container and freeze for a firmer texture.

Per Serving:

Calories: 105; Fat: 0.2g;
Carbohydrates: 27g; Protein: 0.6g

Lychee Sorbet

Serves: 6 ; Prep: 10 Min

Ingredient

- 500g fresh lychees, peeled and pitted
- 100g granulated sugar
- 75ml hot water (60-70°C)

Instruction:

1. In a blender or food processor, combine the peeled and pitted lychees with granulated sugar.
2. Blend until smooth.
3. Add the hot water to the lychee mixture and blend again until well combined.
4. Pour the mixture through a fine-mesh sieve into an empty tub.
5. Place the lid on the tub and freeze for 24 hours.
6. Remove the tub from the freezer and let it sit at room temperature for a few minutes.
7. Select the "SORBET" program on your Ninja CREAMi.
8. Once processing is complete, serve the sorbet immediately or transfer it to a container and freeze for a firmer texture.

Per Serving:

Calories: 120; Fat: 0.4g;
Carbohydrates: 30g; Protein: 1g

CHAPTER 03: SORBET

Guava Sorbet

Serves: 4 ; Prep: 15 Min

Ingredient

- 500g fresh guavas, peeled and seeds removed
- 100g granulated sugar
- 100ml water

Instruction:

1. In a blender, combine the peeled and seeded guavas, granulated sugar, and water. Blend until smooth.
2. Pour the guava mixture through a fine-mesh sieve into an empty tub. Place the lid on the tub and freeze for 24 hours.
3. After 24 hours, remove the tub from the freezer and let it sit at room temperature for a few minutes. Then, follow the quick instructions for assembly and processing according to the "SORBET" program.
4. Select the "SORBET" program on your Ninja CREAMi.
5. Once processing is complete, scoop the sorbet into serving dishes and enjoy immediately.

Per Serving:

Calories: 120; Fat: 0.5g;
Carbohydrates: 30g; Protein: 1g

Plum Sorbet

Serves: 6 ; Prep: 10 Min

Ingredient

- 500g ripe plums, pitted and chopped
- 100g granulated sugar
- 75ml hot water (60-70°C)

Instruction:

1. In a blender or food processor, combine the chopped plums and granulated sugar.
2. Blend until smooth.
3. Add the hot water to the plum mixture and blend again until well combined.
4. Pour the mixture through a fine-mesh sieve into an empty tub.
5. Place the lid on the tub and freeze for 24 hours.
6. Remove the tub from the freezer and let it sit at room temperature for a few minutes.
7. Select the "SORBET" program on your Ninja CREAMi.
8. Once processing is complete, serve the sorbet immediately or transfer it to a container and freeze for a firmer texture.

Per Serving:

Calories: 110; Fat: 0.2g;
Carbohydrates: 28g; Protein: 0.7g

CHAPTER 03: SORBET

Apricot Sorbet

Serves: 6 ; Prep: 10 Min

Ingredient

- 500g ripe apricots, pitted and chopped
- 100g caster sugar
- 75ml hot water (60-70°C)

Instruction:

1. In a blender or food processor, combine the chopped apricots and caster sugar.
2. Blend until smooth.
3. Add the hot water to the apricot mixture and blend again until well combined.
4. Pour the mixture through a fine-mesh sieve into an empty tub.
5. Place the lid on the tub and freeze for 24 hours.
6. Remove the tub from the freezer and let it sit at room temperature for a few minutes.
7. Select the "SORBET" program on your Ninja CREAMi.
8. Once processing is complete, serve the sorbet immediately or transfer it to a container and freeze for a firmer texture.

Per Serving:

Calories: 100; Fat: 0.3g;
Carbohydrates: 25g; Protein: 0.8g

Banana Sorbet

Serves: 4 ; Prep: 10 Min

Ingredient

- 4 ripe bananas, peeled and sliced
- 50g caster sugar
- 50ml hot water (60-70°C)

Instruction:

1. In a blender or food processor, combine the sliced bananas and caster sugar.
2. Blend until smooth.
3. Add the hot water to the banana mixture and blend again until well combined.
4. Pour the mixture through a fine-mesh sieve into an empty tub.
5. Place the lid on the tub and freeze for 24 hours.
6. Remove the tub from the freezer and let it sit at room temperature for a few minutes.
7. Select the "SORBET" program on your Ninja CREAMi.
8. Once processing is complete, serve the sorbet immediately or transfer it to a container and freeze for a firmer texture.

Per Serving:

Calories: 110; Fat: 0.3g;
Carbohydrates: 29g; Protein: 1.3g

CHAPTER 03: SORBET

Fig Sorbet

Serves: 4 ; Prep: 15 Min

Ingredient

- 500g fresh figs, stems removed and quartered
- 100g granulated sugar
- 100ml hot water (60-70°C)

Instruction:

1. In a blender or food processor, combine the quartered figs and granulated sugar.
2. Blend until smooth.
3. Add the hot water to the fig mixture and blend again until well combined.
4. Pour the mixture through a fine-mesh sieve into an empty tub.
5. Place the lid on the tub and freeze for 24 hours.
6. Remove the tub from the freezer and let it sit at room temperature for a few minutes.
7. Select the "SORBET" program on your Ninja CREAMi.
8. Once processing is complete, serve the sorbet immediately or transfer it to a container and freeze for a firmer texture.

Per Serving:

Calories: 150; Fat: 0.3g;
Carbohydrates: 38g; Protein: 1g

Honeydew Melon Sorbet

Serves: 4 ; Prep: 15 Min

Ingredient

- 1 medium honeydew melon, peeled, seeded, and cubed (about 800g)
- 100g granulated sugar
- 100ml hot water (60-70°C)

Instruction:

1. In a blender or food processor, combine the cubed honeydew melon and granulated sugar.
2. Blend until smooth.
3. Add the hot water to the honeydew mixture and blend again until well combined.
4. Pour the mixture through a fine-mesh sieve into an empty tub.
5. Place the lid on the tub and freeze for 24 hours.
6. Remove the tub from the freezer and let it sit at room temperature for a few minutes.
7. Select the "SORBET" program on your Ninja CREAMi.
8. Once processing is complete, serve the sorbet immediately or transfer it to a container and freeze for a firmer texture.

Per Serving:

Calories: 120; Fat: 0.5g;
Carbohydrates: 30g; Protein: 1g

CHAPTER 03: SORBET

Cantaloupe Sorbet

Serves: 4 ; Prep: 15 Min

Ingredient

- 1 medium cantaloupe, peeled, seeded, and cubed (about 800g)
- 100g granulated sugar
- 100ml hot water (60-70°C)

Instruction:

1. In a blender or food processor, combine the cubed cantaloupe and granulated sugar.
2. Blend until smooth.
3. Add the hot water to the cantaloupe mixture and blend again until well combined.
4. Pour the mixture through a fine-mesh sieve into an empty tub.
5. Place the lid on the tub and freeze for 24 hours.
6. Remove the tub from the freezer and let it sit at room temperature for a few minutes.
7. Select the "SORBET" program on your Ninja CREAMi.
8. Once processing is complete, serve the sorbet immediately or transfer it to a container and freeze for a firmer texture.

Per Serving:

Calories: 110; Fat: 0.5g;
Carbohydrates: 28g; Protein: 1g

Tangerine Sorbet

Serves: 4 ; Prep: 15 Min

Ingredient

- 500g tangerines, peeled and seeded
- 100g granulated sugar
- 100ml hot water (60-70°C)

Instruction:

1. In a blender or food processor, combine the peeled and seeded tangerines with the granulated sugar.
2. Blend until smooth.
3. Add the hot water to the tangerine mixture and blend again until well combined.
4. Pour the mixture through a fine-mesh sieve into an empty tub.
5. Place the lid on the tub and freeze for 24 hours.
6. Remove the tub from the freezer and let it sit at room temperature for a few minutes.
7. Select the "SORBET" program on your Ninja CREAMi.
8. Once processing is complete, serve the sorbet immediately or transfer it to a container and freeze for a firmer texture.

Per Serving:

Calories: 120; Fat: 0.2g;
Carbohydrates: 30g; Protein: 1g

CHAPTER 03: SORBET

Mango-Passionfruit Sorbet

Serves: 4 ; Prep: 15 Min

Ingredient

- 2 ripe mangoes, peeled and diced
- Pulp of 4 passionfruits
- 100g granulated sugar
- 100ml hot water (60-70°C)

Instruction:

1. In a blender or food processor, combine the diced mangoes, passionfruit pulp, and granulated sugar.
2. Blend until smooth.
3. Add the hot water to the mango-passionfruit mixture and blend again until well combined.
4. Pour the mixture through a fine-mesh sieve into an empty tub.
5. Place the lid on the tub and freeze for 24 hours.
6. Remove the tub from the freezer and let it sit at room temperature for a few minutes.
7. Select the "SORBET" program on your Ninja CREAMi.
8. Once processing is complete, serve the sorbet immediately or transfer it to a container and freeze for a firmer texture.

Per Serving:

Calories: 160; Fat: 0.5g;
Carbohydrates: 40g; Protein: 1g

Raspberry-Lime Sorbet

Serves: 4 ; Prep: 15 Min

Ingredient

- 300g raspberries
- Zest and juice of 2 limes
- 100g granulated sugar
- 100ml hot water (60-70°C)

Instruction:

1. In a blender or food processor, combine the raspberries, lime zest, lime juice, and granulated sugar.
2. Blend until smooth.
3. Add the hot water to the raspberry-lime mixture and blend again until well combined.
4. Pour the mixture through a fine-mesh sieve into an empty tub.
5. Place the lid on the tub and freeze for 24 hours.
6. Remove the tub from the freezer and let it sit at room temperature for a few minutes.
7. Select the "SORBET" program on your Ninja CREAMi.
8. Once processing is complete, serve the sorbet immediately or transfer it to a container and freeze for a firmer texture.

Per Serving:

Calories: 100; Fat: 0.5g;
Carbohydrates: 25g; Protein: 1g

CHAPTER 03: SORBET

Pomegranate Sorbet

Serves: 4 ; Prep: 15 Min

Ingredient

- 500g fresh pomegranate seeds
- 100g granulated sugar
- 100ml hot water (60-70°C)

Instruction:

1. In a blender or food processor, combine the pomegranate seeds and granulated sugar.
2. Blend until smooth.
3. Add the hot water to the pomegranate mixture and blend again until well combined.
4. Pour the mixture through a fine-mesh sieve into an empty tub.
5. Place the lid on the tub and freeze for 24 hours.
6. Remove the tub from the freezer and let it sit at room temperature for a few minutes.
7. Select the "SORBET" program on your Ninja CREAMi.
8. Once processing is complete, serve the sorbet immediately or transfer it to a container and freeze for a firmer texture.

Per Serving:

Calories: 120; Fat: 0.5g;
Carbohydrates: 30g; Protein: 1g

Vanilla Bean Gelato

Serves: 4 ; Prep: 30 Min

Ingredient

- 3 large egg yolks
- 80g caster sugar
- 200ml whipping cream
- 170ml whole milk
- 1 vanilla bean pod, split and seeds scraped out

Per Serving:

Calories: 250; Fat: 17g;
Carbohydrates: 21g; Protein: 4g

Instruction:

1. In a small saucepan, whisk together the egg yolks and caster sugar until fully combined and sugar is dissolved.
2. Add the whipping cream, whole milk, and scraped vanilla bean seeds to the saucepan. Stir to combine.
3. Place the saucepan on the hob over medium heat, stirring constantly with a whisk or silicone spatula. Cook until the mixture reaches 165-175°F (74-79°C) on an instant-read thermometer.
4. Remove the base from the heat and pour it through a fine-mesh sieve into an empty tub. Place the tub into an ice bath to cool completely.
5. Once cooled, place the lid on the tub and freeze for at least 24 hours.
6. Remove the tub from the freezer and remove the lid from the tub.
7. Select the "GELATO" program on your Ninja CREAMi.
8. Once processing is complete, serve the gelato immediately or transfer it to a container and freeze for a firmer texture.

CHAPTER 04: GELATO

Chocolate Gelato

Serves: 4 ; Prep: 30 Min

Ingredient

- 3 large egg yolks
- 80g caster sugar
- 200ml whipping cream
- 170ml whole milk
- 100g dark chocolate, finely chopped
- Pinch of salt

Per Serving:

Calories: 300; Fat: 20g;
Carbohydrates: 25g; Protein: 5g

Instruction:

1. In a small saucepan, whisk together the egg yolks and caster sugar until fully combined and sugar is dissolved.
2. Add the whipping cream, whole milk, chopped dark chocolate, and salt to the saucepan. Stir to combine.
3. Place the saucepan on the hob over medium heat, stirring constantly with a whisk or silicone spatula. Cook until the mixture reaches 165-175°F (74-79°C) on an instant-read thermometer and the chocolate is completely melted.
4. Remove the base from the heat and pour it through a fine-mesh sieve into an empty tub. Place the tub into an ice bath to cool completely.
5. Once cooled, place the lid on the tub and freeze for at least 24 hours.
6. Remove the tub from the freezer and remove the lid from the tub.
7. Select the "GELATO" program on your Ninja CREAMi.
8. Once processing is complete, serve the gelato immediately or transfer it to a container and freeze for a firmer texture.

Stracciatella Gelato

Serves: 4 ; Prep: 30 Min

Ingredient

- 3 large egg yolks
- 80g caster sugar
- 200ml whipping cream
- 170ml whole milk
- 100g dark chocolate, chopped
- Pinch of salt

Per Serving:

Calories: 300; Fat: 20g; Carbohydrates: 25g; Protein: 5g

Instruction:

1. In a small saucepan, whisk together the egg yolks and caster sugar until fully combined and sugar is dissolved.
2. Add the whipping cream, whole milk, and salt to the saucepan. Stir to combine.
3. Place the saucepan on the hob over medium heat, stirring constantly with a whisk or silicone spatula. Cook until the mixture reaches 165-175°F (74-79°C) on an instant-read thermometer.
4. Remove the base from the heat and pour it through a fine-mesh sieve into an empty tub. Place the tub into an ice bath to cool completely.
5. Once cooled, place the lid on the tub and freeze for at least 24 hours.
6. Remove the tub from the freezer and remove the lid from the tub.
7. Select the "GELATO" program on your Ninja CREAMi.
8. While the gelato is churning, melt the chopped dark chocolate in a heatproof bowl over a pot of simmering water or in the microwave.
9. Once the gelato is almost done churning, drizzle the melted chocolate into the machine in a thin stream to create chocolate shards.
10. Once processing is complete, serve the gelato immediately or transfer it to a container and freeze for a firmer texture.

CHAPTER 04: GELATO

Hazelnut Gelato

Serves: 4 ; Prep: 30 Min

Ingredient

- 3 large egg yolks
- 80g caster sugar
- 200ml whipping cream
- 170ml whole milk
- 100g hazelnuts, toasted and finely ground
- Pinch of salt

Per Serving:

Calories: 320; Fat: 24g; Carbohydrates: 22g; Protein: 6g

Instruction:

1. In a small saucepan, whisk together the egg yolks and caster sugar until fully combined and sugar is dissolved.
2. Add the whipping cream, whole milk, ground hazelnuts, and salt to the saucepan. Stir to combine.
3. Place the saucepan on the hob over medium heat, stirring constantly with a whisk or silicone spatula. Cook until the mixture reaches 165-175°F (74-79°C) on an instant-read thermometer.
4. Remove the base from the heat and pour it through a fine-mesh sieve into an empty tub. Place the tub into an ice bath to cool completely.
5. Once cooled, place the lid on the tub and freeze for at least 24 hours.
6. Remove the tub from the freezer and remove the lid from the tub.
7. Select the "GELATO" program on your Ninja CREAMi.
8. Once processing is complete, serve the gelato immediately or transfer it to a container and freeze for a firmer texture.

Pistachio Gelato

Serves: 4 ; Prep: 30 Min

Ingredient

- 3 large egg yolks
- 80g caster sugar
- 200ml whipping cream
- 170ml whole milk
- 100g pistachios, shelled and finely ground
- Pinch of salt

Per Serving:

Calories: 320; Fat: 24g;
Carbohydrates: 22g; Protein: 6g

Instruction:

1. In a small saucepan, whisk together the egg yolks and caster sugar until fully combined and sugar is dissolved.
2. Add the whipping cream, whole milk, ground pistachios, and salt to the saucepan. Stir to combine.
3. Place the saucepan on the hob over medium heat, stirring constantly with a whisk or silicone spatula. Cook until the mixture reaches 165-175°F (74-79°C) on an instant-read thermometer.
4. Remove the base from the heat and pour it through a fine-mesh sieve into an empty tub. Place the tub into an ice bath to cool completely.
5. Once cooled, place the lid on the tub and freeze for at least 24 hours.
6. Remove the tub from the freezer and remove the lid from the tub.
7. Select the "GELATO" program on your Ninja CREAMi.
8. Once processing is complete, serve the gelato immediately or transfer it to a container and freeze for a firmer texture.

CHAPTER 04: GELATO

Espresso Gelato

Serves: 4 ; Prep: 30 Min

Ingredient

- 3 large egg yolks
- 80g caster sugar
- 200ml whipping cream
- 170ml whole milk
- 2 teaspoons (4g) instant espresso powder
- Pinch of salt

Per Serving:

Calories: 270; Fat: 19g;
Carbohydrates: 20g; Protein: 5g

Instruction:

1. In a small saucepan, whisk together the egg yolks and caster sugar until fully combined and sugar is dissolved.
2. Add the whipping cream, whole milk, instant espresso powder, and salt to the saucepan. Stir to combine.
3. Place the saucepan on the hob over medium heat, stirring constantly with a whisk or silicone spatula. Cook until the mixture reaches 165-175°F (74-79°C) on an instant-read thermometer.
4. Remove the base from the heat and pour it through a fine-mesh sieve into an empty tub. Place the tub into an ice bath to cool completely.
5. Once cooled, place the lid on the tub and freeze for at least 24 hours.
6. Remove the tub from the freezer and remove the lid from the tub.
7. Select the "GELATO" program on your Ninja CREAMi.
8. Once processing is complete, serve the gelato immediately or transfer it to a container and freeze for a firmer texture.

Key Lime Pie Gelato

Serves: 6 ; Prep: 25 Min

Ingredient

- 3 large egg yolks
- 80g caster sugar
- 200ml double cream
- 170ml whole milk
- Zest of 2 limes
- 60ml key lime juice
- 50g crushed graham crackers
- Pinch of salt

Per Serving:

Calories: 210; Fat: 14g;
Carbohydrates: 18g; Protein: 3g

Instruction:

1. In a small saucepan, whisk together the egg yolks and caster sugar until fully combined and sugar is dissolved.
2. Add the double cream, whole milk, lime zest, key lime juice, and pinch of salt to the saucepan. Stir well to combine.
3. Place the saucepan on the hob over medium heat, stirring constantly with a whisk or silicone spatula. Cook until the temperature reaches 165-175°F (74-79°C) on an instant-read thermometer.
4. Remove the base from heat and pour it through a fine-mesh sieve into an empty tub.
5. Place the tub into an ice bath to cool the mixture quickly.
6. Once cooled, place the lid on the tub and freeze for at least 24 hours.
7. Remove the tub from the freezer and let it sit at room temperature for a few minutes.
8. Select the "GELATO" program on your Ninja CREAMi machine.
9. Pour the base into the tub and place it in the machine. Follow the machine's instructions for processing.
10. Once processing is complete, add crushed graham crackers to the gelato and mix gently to incorporate.
11. Serve the gelato immediately or return it to the freezer to firm up further.

CHAPTER 04: GELATO

Cookies and Cream Gelato

Serves: 6 ; Prep: 20 Min

Ingredient

- 3 large egg yolks
- 80g caster sugar
- 200ml double cream
- 170ml whole milk
- 100g chocolate sandwich cookies, crushed
- Pinch of salt

Per Serving:

Calories: 230; Fat: 16g;
Carbohydrates: 18g; Protein: 3g

Instruction:

1. In a small saucepan, whisk together the egg yolks and caster sugar until fully combined and sugar is dissolved.
2. Add the double cream, whole milk, and pinch of salt to the saucepan. Stir well to combine.
3. Place the saucepan on the hob over medium heat, stirring constantly with a whisk or silicone spatula. Cook until the temperature reaches 165-175°F (74-79°C) on an instant-read thermometer.
4. Remove the base from heat and pour it through a fine-mesh sieve into an empty tub.
5. Place the tub into an ice bath to cool the mixture quickly.
6. Once cooled, place the lid on the tub and freeze for at least 24 hours.
7. Remove the tub from the freezer and let it sit at room temperature for a few minutes.
8. Select the "GELATO" program on your Ninja CREAMi machine.
9. Pour the base into the tub and place it in the machine. Follow the machine's instructions for processing.
10. Once processing is complete, add the crushed chocolate sandwich cookies to the gelato and mix gently to incorporate.
11. Serve the gelato immediately or return it to the freezer to firm up further.

Mint Chocolate Chip Gelato

Serves: 6 ; Prep: 15 Min

Ingredient

- 3 large egg yolks
- 80g caster sugar
- 200ml whipping cream
- 170ml whole milk
- 1 teaspoon peppermint extract
- Green food coloring (optional)
- 50g dark chocolate chips

Per Serving:

Calories: 180; Fat: 12g;
Carbohydrates: 15g; Protein: 3g

Instruction:

1. In a small saucepan, whisk together egg yolks and caster sugar until fully combined and sugar is dissolved.
2. Add whipping cream, whole milk, peppermint extract, and green food coloring (if using) to the saucepan. Stir until well combined.
3. Place the saucepan on the hob over medium heat, stirring constantly with a whisk or silicone spatula. Cook until the temperature reaches 165-175°F (74-79°C) on an instant-read thermometer.
4. Remove the base from heat and pour it through a fine-mesh sieve into an empty tub. Place the lid on the tub and freeze for at least 24 hours.
5. After 24 hours, remove the tub from the freezer and take off the lid.
6. Select the "GELATO" program on the Ninja CREAMi.
7. Once processing is complete, add dark chocolate chips during the last few minutes of churning.
8. After mixing, transfer the gelato into a serving dish and enjoy immediately.

CHAPTER 04: GELATO

Almond Gelato

Serves: 6 ; Prep: 15 Min

Ingredient

- 3 large egg yolks
- 80g caster sugar
- 200ml double cream
- 170ml whole milk
- 1 teaspoon almond extract
- 50g chopped almonds

Per Serving:

Calories: 220; Fat: 17g;
Carbohydrates: 13g; Protein: 5g

Instruction:

1. In a small saucepan, whisk together egg yolks and caster sugar until fully combined and sugar is dissolved.
2. Add double cream, whole milk, and almond extract to the saucepan. Stir until well combined.
3. Place the saucepan on the hob over medium heat, stirring constantly with a whisk or silicone spatula. Cook until the temperature reaches 165-175°F (74-79°C) on an instant-read thermometer.
4. Remove the base from heat and pour it through a fine-mesh sieve into an empty tub. Place the lid on the tub and freeze for at least 24 hours.
5. After 24 hours, remove the tub from the freezer and take off the lid.
6. Select the "GELATO" program on the Ninja CREAMi.
7. Once processing is complete, add chopped almonds during the last few minutes of churning.
8. After mixing, transfer the gelato into a serving dish and enjoy immediately.

Coconut Gelato

🍨 Serves: 6 ; Prep: 15 Min

Ingredient

- 3 large egg yolks
- 80g caster sugar
- 200ml double cream
- 170ml coconut milk
- 50g shredded coconut (unsweetened)

Instruction:

1. In a small saucepan, whisk together egg yolks and caster sugar until fully combined and sugar is dissolved.
2. Add double cream and coconut milk to the saucepan. Stir until well combined.
3. Place the saucepan on the hob over medium heat, stirring constantly with a whisk or silicone spatula. Cook until the temperature reaches 165-175°F (74-79°C) on an instant-read thermometer.
4. Remove the base from heat and pour it through a fine-mesh sieve into an empty tub. Stir in shredded coconut. Place the lid on the tub and freeze for at least 24 hours.
5. After 24 hours, remove the tub from the freezer and take off the lid.
6. Select the "GELATO" program on the Ninja CREAMi.
7. Once processing is complete, transfer the gelato into a serving dish and enjoy immediately.

Per Serving:

Calories: 220; Fat: 17g; Carbohydrates: 14g; Protein: 3g

CHAPTER 04: GELATO

Salted Caramel Gelato

🍨 Serves: 6 ; Prep: 15 Min

Ingredient

- 3 large egg yolks
- 80g caster sugar
- 200ml double cream
- 170ml whole milk
- 100g caramel sauce (store-bought or homemade)
- 1/2 teaspoon sea salt

Instruction:

1. In a small saucepan, whisk together egg yolks and caster sugar until fully combined and sugar is dissolved.
2. Add double cream and whole milk to the saucepan. Stir until well combined.
3. Place the saucepan on the hob over medium heat, stirring constantly with a whisk or silicone spatula. Cook until the temperature reaches 165-175°F (74-79°C) on an instant-read thermometer.
4. Remove the base from heat and pour it through a fine-mesh sieve into an empty tub. Stir in caramel sauce and sea salt. Place the lid on the tub and freeze for at least 24 hours.
5. After 24 hours, remove the tub from the freezer and take off the lid.
6. Select the "GELATO" program on the Ninja CREAMi.
7. Once processing is complete, transfer the gelato into a serving dish and enjoy immediately.

Per Serving:

Calories: 230; Fat: 16g; Carbohydrates: 19g; Protein: 3g

Raspberry Ripple Gelato

Serves: 6 ; Prep: 20 Min

Ingredient

- 3 large egg yolks
- 80g caster sugar
- 200ml double cream
- 170ml whole milk
- 150g fresh raspberries
- 50g granulated sugar

Per Serving:

Calories: 250; Fat: 18g; Carbohydrates: 20g; Protein: 3g

Instruction:

1. In a small saucepan, whisk together egg yolks and caster sugar until fully combined and sugar is dissolved.
2. Add double cream and whole milk to the saucepan. Stir until well combined.
3. Place the saucepan on the hob over medium heat, stirring constantly with a whisk or silicone spatula. Cook until the temperature reaches 165-175°F (74-79°C) on an instant-read thermometer.
4. Remove the base from heat and pour it through a fine-mesh sieve into an empty tub. Place the lid on the tub and freeze for at least 24 hours.
5. Meanwhile, in a separate saucepan, combine fresh raspberries and granulated sugar. Cook over medium heat, stirring occasionally, until the raspberries break down and the mixture thickens into a sauce. Remove from heat and let it cool.
6. Once the gelato base is chilled, remove the tub from the freezer and take off the lid.
7. Select the "GELATO" program on the Ninja CREAMi.
8. Once processing is complete, drizzle the raspberry sauce over the gelato and gently swirl it with a spoon or spatula to create the ripple effect.
9. Transfer the gelato into a serving dish and enjoy immediately.

CHAPTER 04: GELATO

Lemon Sorbetto Gelato

Serves: 6 ; Prep: 15 Min

Ingredient

- 200ml water
- 150g granulated sugar
- Zest of 2 lemons
- Juice of 4 lemons
- 1 tablespoon lemon extract

Per Serving:

Calories: 120; Fat: 0g; Carbohydrates: 31g; Protein: 0g

Instruction:

1. In a saucepan, combine water and granulated sugar. Heat over medium heat, stirring until the sugar is dissolved.
2. Add lemon zest to the saucepan and let it simmer for 5 minutes.
3. Remove the saucepan from heat and let the mixture cool to room temperature.
4. Once cooled, stir in lemon juice and lemon extract.
5. Pour the mixture through a fine-mesh sieve into an empty tub. Place the lid on the tub and freeze for at least 24 hours.
6. After 24 hours, remove the tub from the freezer and take off the lid.
7. Select the "GELATO" program on the Ninja CREAMi.
8. Once processing is complete, transfer the sorbetto gelato into a serving dish and enjoy immediately.

Mango Sorbetto Gelato

Serves: 4 ; Prep: 15 Min

Ingredient

- 500g ripe mangoes, peeled and diced
- 150g granulated sugar
- 100ml water
- Juice of 1 lime

Instruction:

1. In a small saucepan, combine granulated sugar and water. Heat over medium heat, stirring until the sugar is dissolved. Let it cool.
2. In a blender, combine diced mangoes, cooled sugar syrup, and lime juice. Blend until smooth.
3. Pour the mixture through a fine-mesh sieve into an empty tub. Place the lid on the tub and freeze for at least 24 hours.
4. After 24 hours, remove the tub from the freezer and take off the lid.
5. Select the "GELATO" program on the Ninja CREAMi.
6. Once processing is complete, transfer the mango sorbetto gelato into a serving dish and enjoy immediately.

Per Serving:

Calories: 140; Fat: 0g;
Carbohydrates: 36g; Protein: 1g

CHAPTER 04: GELATO

Strawberry Sorbetto Gelato

Serves: 6 ; Prep: 15 Min

Ingredient

- 500g fresh strawberries, hulled and halved
- 150g granulated sugar
- 100ml water
- Juice of 1 lemon

Instruction:

1. In a small saucepan, combine granulated sugar and water. Heat over medium heat, stirring until the sugar is dissolved. Let it cool.
2. In a blender, combine halved strawberries, cooled sugar syrup, and lemon juice. Blend until smooth.
3. Pour the mixture through a fine-mesh sieve into an empty tub. Place the lid on the tub and freeze for at least 24 hours.
4. After 24 hours, remove the tub from the freezer and take off the lid.
5. Select the "GELATO" program on the Ninja CREAMi.
6. Once processing is complete, transfer the strawberry sorbetto gelato into a serving dish and enjoy immediately.

Per Serving:

Calories: 120; Fat: 0g;
Carbohydrates: 30g; Protein: 1g

Pistachio Almond Gelato

Serves: 6 ; Prep: 20 Min

Ingredient

- 3 large egg yolks
- 80g caster sugar
- 200ml double cream
- 170ml whole milk
- 50g shelled pistachios
- 50g almond flakes

Per Serving:

Calories: 250; Fat: 18g; Carbohydrates: 15g; Protein: 5g

Instruction:

1. In a small saucepan, whisk together egg yolks and caster sugar until fully combined and sugar is dissolved.
2. Add double cream and whole milk to the saucepan. Stir until well combined.
3. Place the saucepan on the hob over medium heat, stirring constantly with a whisk or silicone spatula. Cook until the temperature reaches 165-175°F (74-79°C) on an instant-read thermometer.
4. Meanwhile, in a food processor, pulse shelled pistachios until finely chopped.
5. Remove the base from heat and pour it through a fine-mesh sieve into an empty tub. Stir in chopped pistachios and almond flakes. Place the lid on the tub and freeze for at least 24 hours.
6. After 24 hours, remove the tub from the freezer and take off the lid.
7. Select the "GELATO" program on the Ninja CREAMi.
8. Once processing is complete, transfer the pistachio almond gelato into a serving dish and enjoy immediately.

CHAPTER 04: GELATO

Dark Chocolate Gelato

Serves: 6 ; Prep: 20 Min

Ingredient

- 3 large egg yolks
- 80g caster sugar
- 200ml double cream
- 170ml whole milk
- 100g dark chocolate (70% cocoa), chopped
- 1 teaspoon vanilla extract

Per Serving:

Calories: 260; Fat: 20g; Carbohydrates: 18g; Protein: 4g

Instruction:

1. In a small saucepan, whisk together egg yolks and caster sugar until fully combined and sugar is dissolved.
2. Add double cream and whole milk to the saucepan. Stir until well combined.
3. Place the saucepan on the hob over medium heat, stirring constantly with a whisk or silicone spatula. Cook until the temperature reaches 165-175°F (74-79°C) on an instant-read thermometer.
4. Meanwhile, in a microwave-safe bowl, melt the dark chocolate in the microwave in 30-second intervals, stirring in between, until smooth.
5. Remove the base from heat and stir in the melted dark chocolate and vanilla extract until well combined.
6. Pour the mixture through a fine-mesh sieve into an empty tub. Place the lid on the tub and freeze for at least 24 hours.
7. After 24 hours, remove the tub from the freezer and take off the lid.
8. Select the "GELATO" program on the Ninja CREAMi.
9. Once processing is complete, transfer the dark chocolate gelato into a serving dish and enjoy immediately.

White Chocolate Raspberry Gelato

Serves: 6 ; Prep: 20 Min

Ingredient

- 3 large egg yolks
- 80g caster sugar
- 200ml double cream
- 170ml whole milk
- 100g white chocolate, chopped
- 100g fresh raspberries

Per Serving:

Calories: 280; Fat: 20g; Carbohydrates: 22g; Protein: 4g

Instruction:

1. In a small saucepan, whisk together egg yolks and caster sugar until fully combined and sugar is dissolved.
2. Add double cream and whole milk to the saucepan. Stir until well combined.
3. Place the saucepan on the hob over medium heat, stirring constantly with a whisk or silicone spatula. Cook until the temperature reaches 165-175°F (74-79°C) on an instant-read thermometer.
4. Meanwhile, in a microwave-safe bowl, melt the white chocolate in the microwave in 30-second intervals, stirring in between, until smooth.
5. Remove the base from heat and stir in the melted white chocolate until well combined.
6. Pour the mixture through a fine-mesh sieve into an empty tub. Place the lid on the tub and freeze for at least 24 hours.
7. After 24 hours, remove the tub from the freezer and take off the lid.
8. Select the "GELATO" program on the Ninja CREAMi.
9. Once processing is complete, add fresh raspberries into the gelato and gently mix.
10. Transfer the white chocolate raspberry gelato into a serving dish and enjoy immediately.

CHAPTER 04: GELATO

Caramel Macchiato Gelato

Serves: 6 ; Prep: 20 Min

Ingredient

- 3 large egg yolks
- 80g caster sugar
- 200ml double cream
- 170ml whole milk
- 2 tablespoons instant coffee granules
- 50g caramel sauce

Per Serving:

Calories: 280; Fat: 20g; Carbohydrates: 22g; Protein: 4g

Instruction:

1. In a small saucepan, whisk together egg yolks and caster sugar until fully combined and sugar is dissolved.
2. Add double cream and whole milk to the saucepan. Stir until well combined.
3. Place the saucepan on the hob over medium heat, stirring constantly with a whisk or silicone spatula. Cook until the temperature reaches 165-175°F (74-79°C) on an instant-read thermometer.
4. Meanwhile, dissolve instant coffee granules in a small amount of hot water to make a strong coffee.
5. Remove the base from heat and stir in the prepared coffee and caramel sauce until well combined.
6. Pour the mixture through a fine-mesh sieve into an empty tub. Place the lid on the tub and freeze for at least 24 hours.
7. After 24 hours, remove the tub from the freezer and take off the lid.
8. Select the "GELATO" program on the Ninja CREAMi.
9. Once processing is complete, transfer the caramel macchiato gelato into a serving dish and enjoy immediately.

Amaretto Gelato

Serves: 6 ; Prep: 20 Min

Ingredient

- 3 large egg yolks
- 80g caster sugar
- 200ml double cream
- 170ml whole milk
- 3 tablespoons amaretto liqueur
- 1 teaspoon almond extract

Per Serving:

Calories: 250; Fat: 18g;
Carbohydrates: 18g; Protein: 4g

Instruction:

1. In a small saucepan, whisk together egg yolks and caster sugar until fully combined and sugar is dissolved.
2. Add double cream and whole milk to the saucepan. Stir until well combined.
3. Place the saucepan on the hob over medium heat, stirring constantly with a whisk or silicone spatula. Cook until the temperature reaches 165-175°F (74-79°C) on an instant-read thermometer.
4. Remove the base from heat and stir in the amaretto liqueur and almond extract until well combined.
5. Pour the mixture through a fine-mesh sieve into an empty tub. Place the lid on the tub and freeze for at least 24 hours.
6. After 24 hours, remove the tub from the freezer and take off the lid.
7. Select the "GELATO" program on the Ninja CREAMi.
8. Once processing is complete, transfer the amaretto gelato into a serving dish and enjoy immediately.

CHAPTER 04: GELATO

Cherry Chocolate Gelato

Serves: 6 ; Prep: 30 Min

Ingredient

- 300g fresh cherries, pitted and halved
- 100g dark chocolate, chopped
- 3 large egg yolks
- 80g caster sugar
- 200ml double cream
- 170ml whole milk

Per Serving:

Calories: 280; Fat: 18g;
Carbohydrates: 25g; Protein: 4g

Instruction:

1. In a small saucepan, whisk together egg yolks and caster sugar until fully combined and sugar is dissolved.
2. Add double cream and whole milk to the saucepan. Stir until well combined.
3. Place the saucepan on the hob over medium heat, stirring constantly with a whisk or silicone spatula. Cook until the temperature reaches 165-175°F (74-79°C) on an instant-read thermometer.
4. Remove the base from heat and let it cool slightly.
5. In a separate bowl, mash the cherries to release their juices.
6. Add the mashed cherries to the gelato base and mix well.
7. Pour the mixture through a fine-mesh sieve into an empty tub. Place the chopped dark chocolate into the mixture.
8. Place the lid on the tub and freeze for at least 24 hours.
9. After 24 hours, remove the tub from the freezer and take off the lid.
10. Select the "GELATO" program on the Ninja CREAMi.
11. Once processing is complete, transfer the cherry chocolate gelato into a serving dish and enjoy immediately.

Peanut Butter Cup Gelato

Serves: 6 ; Prep: 30 Min

Ingredient

- 3 large egg yolks
- 80g caster sugar
- 200ml double cream
- 170ml whole milk
- 100g peanut butter cups, chopped

Instruction:

1. Whisk egg yolks and caster sugar in a small saucepan until fully combined and sugar is dissolved.
2. Add double cream and whole milk to the saucepan. Stir until well combined.
3. Place the saucepan on the hob over medium heat, stirring constantly. Cook until the temperature reaches 165-175°F (74-79°C) on an instant-read thermometer.
4. Remove the base from heat and let it cool slightly.
5. Pour the mixture through a fine-mesh sieve into an empty tub. Add the chopped peanut butter cups to the mixture.
6. Place the lid on the tub and freeze for at least 24 hours.
7. After 24 hours, remove the tub from the freezer and take off the lid.
8. Select the "GELATO" program on the Ninja CREAMi.
9. Once processing is complete, transfer the peanut butter cup gelato into a serving dish and enjoy immediately.

Per Serving:

Calories: 300; Fat: 20g; Carbohydrates: 25g; Protein: 7g

CHAPTER 04: GELATO

Banana Nutella Gelato

Serves: 4 ; Prep: 20 Min

Ingredient

- 3 ripe bananas
- 100g Nutella
- 200ml double cream
- 170ml whole milk
- 50g chopped hazelnuts (optional)

Instruction:

1. Peel and slice the bananas. Place them in a blender along with the Nutella, double cream, and whole milk.
2. Blend the mixture until smooth and well combined.
3. Pour the mixture into a small saucepan and heat over low heat, stirring constantly until it reaches a temperature of 165-175°F (74-79°C) on an instant-read thermometer.
4. Remove the mixture from the heat and let it cool slightly.
5. If using chopped hazelnuts, stir them into the mixture.
6. Pour the mixture through a fine-mesh sieve into an empty tub.
7. Place the tub into an ice bath to cool down completely.
8. Once cooled, place the lid on the tub and freeze for at least 24 hours.
9. After 24 hours, remove the tub from the freezer and take off the lid.
10. Select the "GELATO" program on the Ninja CREAMi and follow the instructions.
11. Once processing is complete, scoop the Banana Nutella gelato into serving dishes and enjoy immediately.

Per Serving:

Calories: 320; Fat: 20g; Carbohydrates: 30g; Protein: 4g

Blueberry Cheesecake Gelato

Serves: 4 ; Prep: 20 Min

Ingredient

- 200g cream cheese
- 200ml double cream
- 170ml whole milk
- 100g fresh blueberries
- 80g caster sugar
- 1 teaspoon vanilla extract
- 50g crushed digestive biscuits (optional)

Per Serving:

Calories: 280; Fat: 20g; Carbohydrates: 22g; Protein: 4g

Instruction:

1. In a blender, combine the cream cheese, double cream, whole milk, fresh blueberries, caster sugar, and vanilla extract. Blend until smooth.
2. Pour the mixture into a saucepan and heat over low heat, stirring continuously until it reaches a temperature of 165-175°F (74-79°C) on an instant-read thermometer.
3. Remove from heat and let the mixture cool down slightly.
4. If using crushed digestive biscuits, stir them into the mixture.
5. Pour the mixture through a fine-mesh sieve into an empty tub.
6. Place the tub into an ice bath to cool completely.
7. Once cooled, place the lid on the tub and freeze for at least 24 hours.
8. After 24 hours, remove the tub from the freezer and take off the lid.
9. Select the "GELATO" program on the Ninja CREAMi and follow the instructions.
10. Once processing is complete, scoop the Blueberry Cheesecake gelato into serving dishes and enjoy immediately.

CHAPTER 04: GELATO

Honey Lavender Gelato

Serves: 6 ; Prep: 30 Min

Ingredient

- 3 large egg yolks
- 80g caster sugar
- 200ml whipping cream
- 170ml whole milk
- 3 tablespoons honey
- 1 tablespoon dried culinary lavender
- Pinch of salt

Per Serving:

Calories: 180; Fat: 12g; Carbohydrates: 15g; Protein: 3g

Instruction:

1. In a small saucepan, whisk together egg yolks and caster sugar until fully combined and sugar is dissolved.
2. Add whipping cream, whole milk, honey, dried lavender, and salt to the saucepan. Stir until well combined.
3. Place the saucepan on the hob over medium heat, stirring constantly with a whisk or silicone spatula. Cook until the temperature reaches 165-175°F (74-79°C) on an instant-read thermometer.
4. Remove the base from heat and pour it through a fine-mesh sieve into an empty tub. Place the lid on the tub and freeze for at least 24 hours.
5. After 24 hours, remove the tub from the freezer and remove the lid.
6. Place the tub into the Ninja CREAMi machine and select the "GELATO" program.
7. Once the processing is complete, add any mix-ins if desired, or simply remove the gelato from the tub and serve immediately.

Orange Creamsicle Gelato

Serves: 6 ; Prep: 30 Min

Ingredient

- 3 large egg yolks
- 80g caster sugar
- 200ml whipping cream
- 170ml whole milk
- Zest of 2 oranges
- 120ml freshly squeezed orange juice
- Pinch of salt

Per Serving:

Calories: 150; Fat: 10g;
Carbohydrates: 13g; Protein: 3g

Instruction:

1. Whisk egg yolks and caster sugar in a small saucepan until sugar dissolves.
2. Add whipping cream, whole milk, orange zest, orange juice, and salt. Stir well.
3. Heat mixture on medium heat, stirring constantly, until it reaches 165-175°F (74-79°C).
4. Remove from heat and pour through a sieve into an empty tub. Freeze for 24 hours.
5. After freezing, remove tub from freezer and lid from tub.
6. Place the tub in the Ninja CREAMi machine and select the "GELATO" program.
7. Once processing is complete, add mix-ins if desired, or serve immediately.

CHAPTER 04: GELATO

Coconut Lime Gelato

Serves: 6 ; Prep: 30 Min

Ingredient

- 3 large egg yolks
- 80g caster sugar
- 200ml whipping cream
- 170ml whole milk
- Zest of 2 limes
- 120ml coconut milk
- Pinch of salt

Per Serving:

Calories: 170; Fat: 12g;
Carbohydrates: 12g; Protein: 3g

Instruction:

1. Whisk egg yolks and caster sugar in a small saucepan until sugar dissolves.
2. Add whipping cream, whole milk, lime zest, coconut milk, and salt. Stir well.
3. Heat mixture on medium heat, stirring constantly, until it reaches 165-175°F (74-79°C).
4. Remove from heat and pour through a sieve into an empty tub. Freeze for 24 hours.
5. After freezing, remove tub from freezer and lid from tub.
6. Place the tub in the Ninja CREAMi machine and select the "GELATO" program.
7. Once processing is complete, add mix-ins if desired, or serve immediately.

Black Forest Gelato

Serves: 6 ; Prep: 30 Min

Ingredient

- 3 large egg yolks
- 80g caster sugar
- 200ml whipping cream
- 170ml whole milk
- 50g dark chocolate, chopped
- 50g cherries, pitted and chopped
- 1 tablespoon cherry liqueur (optional)
- Pinch of salt

Per Serving:

Calories: 220; Fat: 16g;
Carbohydrates: 15g; Protein: 4g

Instruction:

1. Whisk egg yolks and caster sugar in a small saucepan until sugar dissolves.
2. Add whipping cream, whole milk, chopped dark chocolate, chopped cherries, cherry liqueur (if using), and salt. Stir well.
3. Heat mixture on medium heat, stirring constantly, until it reaches 165-175°F (74-79°C).
4. Remove from heat and pour through a sieve into an empty tub. Freeze for 24 hours.
5. After freezing, remove tub from freezer and lid from tub.
6. Place the tub in the Ninja CREAMi machine and select the "GELATO" program.
7. Once processing is complete, serve immediately.

CHAPTER 04: GELATO

Mango Tango Gelato

Serves: 6 ; Prep: 30 Min

Ingredient

- 3 large egg yolks
- 80g caster sugar
- 200ml whipping cream
- 170ml whole milk
- 300g ripe mango, peeled and diced
- 1 tablespoon lime juice
- Pinch of salt

Per Serving:

Calories: 180; Fat: 10g;
Carbohydrates: 20g; Protein: 4g

Instruction:

1. Whisk egg yolks and caster sugar in a small saucepan until sugar dissolves.
2. Add whipping cream, whole milk, diced mango, lime juice, and salt. Stir well.
3. Heat mixture on medium heat, stirring constantly, until it reaches 165-175°F (74-79°C).
4. Remove from heat and pour through a sieve into an empty tub. Freeze for 24 hours.
5. After freezing, remove tub from freezer and lid from tub.
6. Place the tub in the Ninja CREAMi machine and select the "GELATO" program.
7. Once processing is complete, serve immediately.

Pineapple Coconut Gelato

Serves: 6 ; Prep: 30 Min

Ingredient

- 3 large egg yolks
- 80g caster sugar
- 200ml whipping cream
- 170ml whole milk
- 200g pineapple chunks
- 120ml coconut milk
- Pinch of salt

Per Serving:

Calories: 200; Fat: 14g;
Carbohydrates: 16g; Protein: 4g

Instruction:

1. Whisk egg yolks and caster sugar in a small saucepan until sugar dissolves.
2. Add whipping cream, whole milk, pineapple chunks, coconut milk, and salt. Stir well.
3. Heat mixture on medium heat, stirring constantly, until it reaches 165-175°F (74-79°C).
4. Remove from heat and pour through a sieve into an empty tub. Freeze for 24 hours.
5. After freezing, remove tub from freezer and lid from tub.
6. Place the tub in the Ninja CREAMi machine and select the "GELATO" program.
7. Once processing is complete, serve immediately.

CHAPTER 04: GELATO

Cinnamon Roll Gelato

Serves: 6 ; Prep: 30 Min

Ingredient

- 3 large egg yolks
- 80g caster sugar
- 200ml whipping cream
- 170ml whole milk
- 2 teaspoons ground cinnamon
- 50g brown sugar
- 50g chopped pecans (optional)
- Pinch of salt

Per Serving:

Calories: 210; Fat: 15g;
Carbohydrates: 17g; Protein: 4g

Instruction:

1. Whisk egg yolks and caster sugar in a small saucepan until sugar dissolves.
2. Add whipping cream, whole milk, ground cinnamon, brown sugar, chopped pecans (if using), and salt. Stir well.
3. Heat mixture on medium heat, stirring constantly, until it reaches 165-175°F (74-79°C).
4. Remove from heat and pour through a sieve into an empty tub. Freeze for 24 hours.
5. After freezing, remove tub from freezer and lid from tub.
6. Place the tub in the Ninja CREAMi machine and select the "GELATO" program.
7. Once processing is complete, serve immediately.

Mixed Berry Smoothie Bowl

Serves: 2 ; Prep: 5 Min

Ingredient

- 120g mixed berries (such as strawberries, blueberries, raspberries)
- 75g ripe, peeled banana, sliced
- 150 ml yogurt
- 100 ml whole milk
- Toppings (optional): Sliced bananas, Mixed berry slices, Granola

Per Serving:

Calories: 120; Fat: 3g;
Carbohydrates: 20g; Protein: 5g

Instruction:

1. Fill an empty container with mixed berries and banana slices.
2. Cover the fruit with yogurt and milk. Place the lid on the tub and freeze for 24 hours.
3. Remove the tub from the freezer and remove the lid. Follow the quick instructions for assembly and processing.
4. Select the SMOOTHIE BOWL program.
5. Once processing is complete, transfer the processed base to a bowl and top with sliced bananas, mixed berries, and granola.

CHAPTER 05: SMOOTHIE BOWL

Tropical Mango Smoothie Bowl

Serves: 2 ; Prep: 5 Min

Ingredient

- 150g mango chunks
- 75g ripe, peeled banana, sliced
- 150 ml coconut milk
- 50 ml orange juice
- Toppings (optional): Sliced mango, Toasted coconut flakes, Chia seeds

Per Serving:

Calories: 180; Fat: 8g;
Carbohydrates: 25g; Protein: 3g

Instruction:

1. Fill an empty container with mango chunks and banana slices.
2. Pour in coconut milk and orange juice. Place the lid on the tub and freeze for 24 hours.
3. Remove the tub from the freezer and take off the lid. Follow the quick instructions for assembly and processing.
4. Select the SMOOTHIE BOWL program.
5. Once processing is complete, transfer the processed base to a bowl and top with sliced mango, toasted coconut flakes, and chia seeds.

Strawberry Banana Smoothie Bowl

Serves: 2 ; Prep: 5 Min

Ingredient

- 120g strawberries, thinly sliced
- 75g ripe banana, peeled and sliced
- 150 ml yogurt
- 100 ml whole milk
- Optional Toppings: Banana chips, Strawberry slices, Roasted flaked almonds

Per Serving:

Calories: 150; Fat: 4g;
Carbohydrates: 25g; Protein: 6g

Instruction:

1. Arrange the sliced strawberries and bananas in an empty container.
2. Pour yogurt and whole milk over the fruit, ensuring they are fully covered. Place the lid on the tub and freeze for 24 hours.
3. Remove the tub from the freezer and take off the lid. Follow the quick instructions for assembly and processing.
4. Select the SMOOTHIE BOWL program.
5. Once processing is complete, transfer the processed base to a bowl and garnish with your preferred toppings.

CHAPTER 05: SMOOTHIE BOWL

Blueberry Acai Smoothie Bowl

Serves: 2 ; Prep: 5 Min

Ingredient

- 120g blueberries
- 50g acai berry puree
- 75g ripe banana, peeled and sliced
- 150 ml yogurt
- 100 ml whole milk
- Optional Toppings: Sliced bananas, Granola, Chia seeds

Per Serving:

Calories: 160; Fat: 4g;
Carbohydrates: 25g; Protein: 6g

Instruction:

1. Add blueberries, acai berry puree, and sliced banana to an empty container.
2. Pour yogurt and whole milk over the fruit mixture, ensuring they are fully covered. Place the lid on the tub and freeze for 24 hours.
3. Remove the tub from the freezer and take off the lid. Follow the quick instructions for assembly and processing.
4. Select the SMOOTHIE BOWL program.
5. Once processing is complete, transfer the processed base to a bowl and top with sliced bananas, granola, and chia seeds.

Peanut Butter Banana Smoothie Bowl

Serves: 2 ; Prep: 5 Min

Ingredient

- 75g ripe banana, peeled and sliced
- 30g peanut butter
- 150 ml yogurt
- 100 ml whole milk
- Optional Toppings: Sliced bananas, Peanut butter drizzle, Granola

Per Serving:

Calories: 250; Fat: 12g;
Carbohydrates: 25g; Protein: 10g

Instruction:

1. Place sliced banana and peanut butter in an empty container.
2. Pour yogurt and whole milk over the banana and peanut butter, ensuring they are fully covered. Place the lid on the tub and freeze for 24 hours.
3. Remove the tub from the freezer and take off the lid. Follow the quick instructions for assembly and processing.
4. Select the SMOOTHIE BOWL program.
5. Once processing is complete, transfer the processed base to a bowl and top with sliced bananas, a drizzle of peanut butter, and granola.

CHAPTER 05: SMOOTHIE BOWL

Green Goddess Smoothie Bowl

Serves: 2 ; Prep: 5 Min

Ingredient

- 100g spinach leaves
- 1 ripe avocado, peeled and pitted
- 1 ripe banana, peeled and sliced
- 150 ml coconut water
- 50 ml Greek yogurt
- Optional Toppings: Sliced kiwi, Chia seeds, Toasted coconut flakes

Per Serving:

Calories: 200; Fat: 12g;
Carbohydrates: 20g; Protein: 5g

Instruction:

1. Add spinach leaves, avocado, and sliced banana to an empty container.
2. Pour in coconut water and Greek yogurt. Ensure ingredients are fully covered. Place the lid on the tub and freeze for 24 hours.
3. Remove the tub from the freezer and take off the lid. Follow the quick instructions for assembly and processing.
4. Select the SMOOTHIE BOWL program.
5. Once processing is complete, transfer the processed base to a bowl and garnish with sliced kiwi, chia seeds, and toasted coconut flakes.

Chocolate Peanut Butter Smoothie Bowl

Serves: 2 ; Prep: 5 Min

Ingredient

- 30g cocoa powder
- 30g peanut butter
- 1 ripe banana, peeled and sliced
- 150 ml almond milk
- 50 ml Greek yogurt
- Optional Toppings: Sliced banana, Chocolate chips, Peanut butter drizzle

Instruction:

1. Add cocoa powder, peanut butter, and sliced banana to an empty container.
2. Pour in almond milk and Greek yogurt. Ensure ingredients are fully covered. Place the lid on the tub and freeze for 24 hours.
3. Remove the tub from the freezer and take off the lid. Follow the quick instructions for assembly and processing.
4. Select the SMOOTHIE BOWL program.
5. Once processing is complete, transfer the processed base to a bowl and top with sliced banana, chocolate chips, and a drizzle of peanut butter.

Per Serving:

Calories: 200; Fat: 10g;
Carbohydrates: 25g; Protein: 7g

CHAPTER 05: SMOOTHIE BOWL

Peach Raspberry Smoothie Bowl

Serves: 2 ; Prep: 5 Min

Ingredient

- 120g raspberries
- 100g peach slices
- 150 ml yogurt
- 100 ml coconut water
- Optional Toppings: Sliced peaches, Fresh raspberries, Granola

Instruction:

1. Add raspberries and peach slices to an empty container.
2. Pour in yogurt and coconut water. Ensure ingredients are fully covered. Place the lid on the tub and freeze for 24 hours.
3. Remove the tub from the freezer and take off the lid. Follow the quick instructions for assembly and processing.
4. Select the SMOOTHIE BOWL program.
5. Once processing is complete, transfer the processed base to a bowl and top with sliced peaches, fresh raspberries, and granola.

Per Serving:

Calories: 120; Fat: 2g;
Carbohydrates: 25g; Protein: 3g

Kiwi Coconut Smoothie Bowl

Serves: 2 ; Prep: 5 Min

Ingredient

- 100g kiwi, peeled and sliced
- 30g shredded coconut
- 150 ml coconut milk
- 50 ml Greek yogurt
- Optional Toppings: Sliced kiwi, Toasted coconut flakes, Chia seeds

Instruction:

1. Place sliced kiwi and shredded coconut in an empty container.
2. Pour in coconut milk and Greek yogurt. Ensure ingredients are fully covered. Place the lid on the tub and freeze for 24 hours.
3. Remove the tub from the freezer and take off the lid. Follow the quick instructions for assembly and processing.
4. Select the SMOOTHIE BOWL program.
5. Once processing is complete, transfer the processed base to a bowl and garnish with sliced kiwi, toasted coconut flakes, and chia seeds.

Per Serving:

Calories: 200; Fat: 10g;
Carbohydrates: 20g; Protein: 5g

CHAPTER 05: SMOOTHIE BOWL

Pineapple Spinach Smoothie Bowl

Serves: 2 ; Prep: 5 Min

Ingredient

- 100g pineapple chunks
- 50g spinach leaves
- 150 ml coconut water
- 50 ml Greek yogurt
- Optional Toppings: Sliced pineapple, Toasted coconut flakes, Chia seeds

Instruction:

1. Add pineapple chunks and spinach leaves to an empty container.
2. Pour in coconut water and Greek yogurt. Ensure ingredients are fully covered. Place the lid on the tub and freeze for 24 hours.
3. Remove the tub from the freezer and take off the lid. Follow the quick instructions for assembly and processing.
4. Select the SMOOTHIE BOWL program.
5. Once processing is complete, transfer the processed base to a bowl and top with sliced pineapple, toasted coconut flakes, and chia seeds.

Per Serving:

Calories: 100; Fat: 2g;
Carbohydrates: 20g; Protein: 5g

Cherry Almond Smoothie Bowl

Serves: 2 ; Prep: 5 Min

Ingredient

- 120g cherries, pitted
- 30g almonds, chopped
- 150 ml almond milk
- 50 ml Greek yogurt
- Optional Toppings: Sliced cherries, Toasted almond slices, Honey drizzle

Instruction:

1. Place pitted cherries and chopped almonds in an empty container.
2. Pour in almond milk and Greek yogurt. Ensure ingredients are fully covered. Place the lid on the tub and freeze for 24 hours.
3. Remove the tub from the freezer and take off the lid. Follow the quick instructions for assembly and processing.
4. Select the SMOOTHIE BOWL program.
5. Once processing is complete, transfer the processed base to a bowl and top with sliced cherries, toasted almond slices, and a drizzle of honey.

Per Serving:

Calories: 150; Fat: 8g;
Carbohydrates: 15g; Protein: 5g

CHAPTER 05: SMOOTHIE BOWL

Watermelon Mint Smoothie Bowl

Serves: 2 ; Prep: 5 Min

Ingredient

- 200g watermelon, diced
- 10g fresh mint leaves
- 150 ml coconut water
- 50 ml Greek yogurt
- Optional Toppings: Watermelon balls, Fresh mint leaves, Coconut flakes

Instruction:

1. Place diced watermelon and fresh mint leaves in an empty container.
2. Pour in coconut water and Greek yogurt. Ensure ingredients are fully covered. Place the lid on the tub and freeze for 24 hours.
3. Remove the tub from the freezer and take off the lid. Follow the quick instructions for assembly and processing.
4. Select the SMOOTHIE BOWL program.
5. Once processing is complete, transfer the processed base to a bowl and garnish with watermelon balls, fresh mint leaves, and coconut flakes.

Per Serving:

Calories: 70; Fat: 1g;
Carbohydrates: 15g; Protein: 3g

Raspberry Lime Smoothie Bowl

Serves: 2 ; Prep: 5 Min

Ingredient

- 120g raspberries
- Juice of 1 lime
- 150 ml coconut water
- 50 ml Greek yogurt
- Optional Toppings: Fresh raspberries, Lime slices, Coconut flakes

Instruction:

1. Add raspberries and lime juice to an empty container.
2. Pour in coconut water and Greek yogurt. Ensure ingredients are fully covered. Place the lid on the tub and freeze for 24 hours.
3. Remove the tub from the freezer and take off the lid. Follow the quick instructions for assembly and processing.
4. Select the SMOOTHIE BOWL program.
5. Once processing is complete, transfer the processed base to a bowl and garnish with fresh raspberries, lime slices, and coconut flakes.

Per Serving:

Calories: 60; Fat: 1g;
Carbohydrates: 15g; Protein: 3g

CHAPTER 05: SMOOTHIE BOWL

Mango Pineapple Smoothie Bowl

Serves: 2 ; Prep: 5 Min

Ingredient

- 150g mango chunks
- 100g pineapple chunks
- 150 ml coconut milk
- 50 ml Greek yogurt
- Optional Toppings: Sliced mango, Pineapple chunks, Coconut flakes

Instruction:

1. Place mango chunks and pineapple chunks in an empty container.
2. Pour in coconut milk and Greek yogurt. Ensure ingredients are fully covered. Place the lid on the tub and freeze for 24 hours.
3. Remove the tub from the freezer and take off the lid. Follow the quick instructions for assembly and processing.
4. Select the SMOOTHIE BOWL program.
5. Once processing is complete, transfer the processed base to a bowl and top with sliced mango, pineapple chunks, and coconut flakes.

Per Serving:

Calories: 120; Fat: 4g;
Carbohydrates: 20g; Protein: 3g

Dragon Fruit Smoothie Bowl

Serves: 2 ; Prep: 5 Min

Ingredient

- 150g dragon fruit flesh, diced
- 100g mixed berries (such as strawberries, blueberries, raspberries)
- 150 ml almond milk
- 50 ml Greek yogurt
- Optional Toppings: Sliced dragon fruit, Mixed berries, Granola

Per Serving:

Calories: 100; Fat: 2g;
Carbohydrates: 20g; Protein: 3g

Instruction:

1. Place diced dragon fruit and mixed berries in an empty container.
2. Pour in almond milk and Greek yogurt. Ensure ingredients are fully covered. Place the lid on the tub and freeze for 24 hours.
3. Remove the tub from the freezer and take off the lid. Follow the quick instructions for assembly and processing.
4. Select the SMOOTHIE BOWL program.
5. Once processing is complete, transfer the processed base to a bowl and top with sliced dragon fruit, mixed berries, and granola.

CHAPTER 05: SMOOTHIE BOWL

Orange Carrot Smoothie Bowl

Serves: 2 ; Prep: 5 Min

Ingredient

- 150g carrots, peeled and chopped
- 1 large orange, peeled and segmented
- 150 ml orange juice
- 50 ml Greek yogurt
- Optional Toppings: Sliced oranges, Shredded carrots, Chia seeds

Per Serving:

Calories: 90; Fat: 1g;
Carbohydrates: 20g; Protein: 3g

Instruction:

1. Place chopped carrots and orange segments in an empty container.
2. Pour in orange juice and Greek yogurt. Ensure ingredients are fully covered. Place the lid on the tub and freeze for 24 hours.
3. Remove the tub from the freezer and take off the lid. Follow the quick instructions for assembly and processing.
4. Select the SMOOTHIE BOWL program.
5. Once processing is complete, transfer the processed base to a bowl and top with sliced oranges, shredded carrots, and chia seeds.

Beet Berry Smoothie Bowl

Serves: 2 ; Prep: 5 Min

Ingredient

- 100g cooked beets, chopped
- 100g mixed berries (such as strawberries, raspberries, blueberries)
- 150 ml almond milk
- 50 ml Greek yogurt
- Optional Toppings: Fresh berries, Granola, Shredded coconut

Per Serving:

Calories: 100; Fat: 2g;
Carbohydrates: 18g; Protein: 3g

Instruction:

1. Place chopped cooked beets and mixed berries in an empty container.
2. Pour in almond milk and Greek yogurt. Ensure ingredients are fully covered. Place the lid on the tub and freeze for 24 hours.
3. Remove the tub from the freezer and take off the lid. Follow the quick instructions for assembly and processing.
4. Select the SMOOTHIE BOWL program.
5. Once processing is complete, transfer the processed base to a bowl and top with fresh berries, granola, and shredded coconut.

CHAPTER 05: SMOOTHIE BOWL

Avocado Blueberry Smoothie Bowl

Serves: 2 ; Prep: 5 Min

Ingredient

- 1 ripe avocado, peeled and pitted
- 100g blueberries
- 150 ml almond milk
- 50 ml Greek yogurt
- Optional Toppings: Sliced bananas, Chia seeds, Honey drizzle

Per Serving:

Calories: 150; Fat: 10g;
Carbohydrates: 15g; Protein: 4g

Instruction:

1. Place ripe avocado and blueberries in an empty container.
2. Pour in almond milk and Greek yogurt. Ensure ingredients are fully covered. Place the lid on the tub and freeze for 24 hours.
3. Remove the tub from the freezer and take off the lid. Follow the quick instructions for assembly and processing.
4. Select the SMOOTHIE BOWL program.
5. Once processing is complete, transfer the processed base to a bowl and top with sliced bananas, chia seeds, and a drizzle of honey.

Blackberry Banana Smoothie Bowl

Serves: 2 ; Prep: 5 Min

Ingredient

- 150g blackberries
- 1 ripe banana, sliced
- 150 ml natural yogurt
- 50 ml almond milk
- Optional Toppings: Sliced bananas, Granola, Shredded coconut

Instruction:

1. Arrange blackberries and sliced banana in an empty container.
2. Pour natural yogurt and almond milk over the fruit. Ensure everything is covered. Place the lid on the tub and freeze for 24 hours.
3. Remove the tub from the freezer and take off the lid. Follow the quick instructions for assembly and processing.
4. Select the SMOOTHIE BOWL program.
5. Once processing is complete, transfer the processed base to a bowl and top with sliced bananas, granola, and shredded coconut.

Per Serving:

Calories: 120; Fat: 2g;
Carbohydrates: 24g; Protein: 3g

CHAPTER 05: SMOOTHIE BOWL

Strawberry Kiwi Smoothie Bowl

Serves: 2 ; Prep: 5 Min

Ingredient

- 150g strawberries, sliced
- 2 kiwis, peeled and sliced
- 150 ml yogurt
- 50 ml coconut water
- Optional Toppings: Sliced kiwi, Granola, Chia seeds

Instruction:

1. Arrange sliced strawberries and kiwis in an empty container.
2. Pour yogurt and coconut water over the fruit. Ensure everything is covered. Place the lid on the tub and freeze for 24 hours.
3. Remove the tub from the freezer and take off the lid. Follow the quick instructions for assembly and processing.
4. Select the SMOOTHIE BOWL program.
5. Once processing is complete, transfer the processed base to a bowl and top with sliced kiwi, granola, and chia seeds.

Per Serving:

Calories: 120; Fat: 2g;
Carbohydrates: 24g; Protein: 3g

Raspberry Peach Smoothie Bowl

Serves: 2 ; Prep: 5 Min

Ingredient

- 150g raspberries
- 2 ripe peaches, sliced
- 150 ml yogurt
- 50 ml almond milk
- Optional Toppings: Sliced peaches, Granola, Shredded coconut

Per Serving:

Calories: 120; Fat: 2g;
Carbohydrates: 24g; Protein: 3g

Instruction:

1. Arrange raspberries and sliced peaches in an empty container.
2. Pour yogurt and almond milk over the fruit. Ensure everything is covered. Place the lid on the tub and freeze for 24 hours.
3. Remove the tub from the freezer and take off the lid. Follow the quick instructions for assembly and processing.
4. Select the SMOOTHIE BOWL program.
5. Once processing is complete, transfer the processed base to a bowl and top with sliced peaches, granola, and shredded coconut.

CHAPTER 05: SMOOTHIE BOWL

Chocolate Cherry Smoothie Bowl

Serves: 2 ; Prep: 5 Min

Ingredient

- 150g cherries, pitted
- 2 tablespoons cocoa powder
- 150 ml Greek yogurt
- 50 ml almond milk
- Optional Toppings: Dark chocolate chips, Sliced almonds, Fresh cherries

Per Serving:

Calories: 160; Fat: 5g;
Carbohydrates: 22g; Protein: 8g

Instruction:

1. Place the pitted cherries, cocoa powder, Greek yogurt, and almond milk into the empty container.
2. Ensure all ingredients are well combined. Place the lid on the tub and freeze for 24 hours.
3. Remove the tub from the freezer and take off the lid. Follow the quick instructions for assembly and processing.
4. Select the SMOOTHIE BOWL program.
5. Once processing is complete, transfer the processed base to a bowl and top with dark chocolate chips, sliced almonds, and fresh cherries.

Apple Cinnamon Smoothie Bowl

Serves: 2 ; Prep: 5 Min

Ingredient

- 2 medium apples, cored and sliced
- 1 teaspoon ground cinnamon
- 150 ml Greek yogurt
- 50 ml almond milk
- Optional Toppings: Granola, Sliced almonds, Honey drizzle

Instruction:

1. Place the sliced apples, ground cinnamon, Greek yogurt, and almond milk into the empty container.
2. Ensure all ingredients are well combined. Place the lid on the tub and freeze for 24 hours.
3. Remove the tub from the freezer and take off the lid. Follow the quick instructions for assembly and processing.
4. Select the SMOOTHIE BOWL program.
5. Once processing is complete, transfer the processed base to a bowl and top with granola, sliced almonds, and a drizzle of honey.

Per Serving:

Calories: 120; Fat: 3g;
Carbohydrates: 22g; Protein: 5g

CHAPTER 05: SMOOTHIE BOWL

Pina Colada Smoothie Bowl

Serves: 2 ; Prep: 5 Min

Ingredient

- 200g frozen pineapple chunks
- 100ml coconut milk
- 100ml Greek yogurt
- 1 tablespoon honey (optional)
- Shredded coconut, pineapple slices, and mint leaves for topping

Instruction:

1. Place the frozen pineapple chunks, coconut milk, Greek yogurt, and honey (if using) into the empty container.
2. Make sure all ingredients are well combined. Place the lid on the tub and freeze for 24 hours.
3. Remove the tub from the freezer and take off the lid. Follow the quick instructions for assembly and processing.
4. Select the SMOOTHIE BOWL program.
5. Once processing is complete, transfer the processed base to a bowl and top with shredded coconut, pineapple slices, and mint leaves.

Per Serving:

Calories: 160; Fat: 9g;
Carbohydrates: 19g; Protein: 3g

Strawberry Milkshake

Serves: 1 ; Prep: 5 Min

Ingredient

- 200g vanilla ice cream
- 85 ml whole milk
- 100 g fresh strawberries, stems removed and halved

Instruction:

1. Add vanilla ice cream, whole milk, and fresh strawberries to the empty container in the order listed.
2. Follow the quick instructions for assembly and processing.
3. Select the MILKSHAKE program.
4. Once processing is complete, add "Mix-Ins" or "RE-SPIN" if necessary. Then remove the milkshake from the tub and serve immediately.

Per Serving:

Calories: 280; Fat: 15g;
Carbohydrates: 30g; Protein: 6g

CHAPTER 06: MILKSHAKE

Cookies and Cream Milkshake

Serves: 1 ; Prep: 5 Min

Ingredient

- 200g vanilla ice cream
- 85 ml whole milk
- 2 Oreo cookies, crushed

Instruction:

1. Add vanilla ice cream, whole milk, and crushed Oreo cookies to the empty container in the order listed.
2. Follow the quick instructions for assembly and processing.
3. Select the MILKSHAKE program.
4. Once processing is complete, add "Mix-Ins" or "RE-SPIN" if necessary. Then remove the milkshake from the tub and serve immediately.

Per Serving:

Calories: 380; Fat: 20g;
Carbohydrates: 40g; Protein: 7g

Mint Chocolate Chip Milkshake

Serves: 1 ; Prep: 5 Min

Ingredient

- 200g vanilla ice cream
- 85 ml whole milk
- 1 tablespoon chocolate chips
- 1/4 teaspoon mint extract

Instruction:

1. Add vanilla ice cream, whole milk, chocolate chips, and mint extract to the empty container in the order listed.
2. Follow the quick instructions for assembly and processing.
3. Select the MILKSHAKE program.
4. Once processing is complete, add "Mix-Ins" or "RE-SPIN" if necessary. Then remove the milkshake from the tub and serve immediately.

Per Serving:

Calories: 430; Fat: 24g;
Carbohydrates: 48g; Protein: 7g

CHAPTER 06: MILKSHAKE

Peanut Butter Cup Milkshake

Serves: 1 ; Prep: 5 Min

Ingredient

- 200g vanilla ice cream
- 85 ml whole milk
- 2 tablespoons peanut butter
- 2 tablespoons chocolate syrup

Instruction:

1. Add vanilla ice cream, whole milk, peanut butter, and chocolate syrup to the empty container in the order listed.
2. Follow the quick instructions for assembly and processing.
3. Select the MILKSHAKE program.
4. Once processing is complete, add "Mix-Ins" or "RE-SPIN" if necessary. Then remove the milkshake from the tub and serve immediately.

Per Serving:

Calories: 550; Fat: 35g;
Carbohydrates: 46g; Protein: 15g

Banana Split Milkshake

Serves: 1 ; Prep: 5 Min

Ingredient

- 200g vanilla ice cream
- 85 ml whole milk
- 1 ripe banana, peeled and sliced
- 2 tablespoons chocolate syrup
- 2 tablespoons strawberry syrup
- Whipped cream, for topping
- Maraschino cherry, for garnish
- Sprinkles, for garnish
- Chopped nuts, for garnish

Instruction:

1. Add vanilla ice cream, whole milk, sliced banana, chocolate syrup, and strawberry syrup to the empty container in the order listed.
2. Follow the quick instructions for assembly and processing.
3. Select the MILKSHAKE program.
4. Once processing is complete, add whipped cream on top and garnish with a maraschino cherry, sprinkles, and chopped nuts.
5. Serve immediately.

Per Serving:

Calories: 550; Fat: 22g;
Carbohydrates: 85g; Protein: 8g

CHAPTER 06: MILKSHAKE

Salted Caramel Milkshake

Serves: 1 ; Prep: 5 Min

Ingredient

- 200g vanilla ice cream
- 85 ml whole milk
- 2 tablespoons salted caramel sauce
- Whipped cream, for topping
- Caramel sauce, for drizzling
- Sea salt, for garnish

Instruction:

1. Add vanilla ice cream, whole milk, and salted caramel sauce to the empty container in the order listed.
2. Follow the quick instructions for assembly and processing.
3. Select the MILKSHAKE program.
4. Once processing is complete, add whipped cream on top and drizzle with caramel sauce.
5. Garnish with a sprinkle of sea salt.
6. Serve immediately.

Per Serving:

Calories: 520; Fat: 23g;
Carbohydrates: 68g; Protein: 9g

Chocolate Peanut Butter Milkshake

Serves: 1 ; Prep: 5 Min

Ingredient

- 200g chocolate ice cream
- 85 ml whole milk
- 2 tablespoons peanut butter
- Whipped cream, for topping
- Chocolate syrup, for drizzling
- Chopped peanuts, for garnish

Instruction:

1. Add chocolate ice cream, whole milk, and peanut butter to the empty container in the order listed.
2. Follow the quick instructions for assembly and processing.
3. Select the MILKSHAKE program.
4. Once processing is complete, add whipped cream on top and drizzle with chocolate syrup.
5. Garnish with chopped peanuts.
6. Serve immediately.

Per Serving:

Calories: 590; Fat: 35g;
Carbohydrates: 56g; Protein: 14g

CHAPTER 06: MILKSHAKE

Oreo Milkshake

Serves: 1 ; Prep: 5 Min

Ingredient

- 200g vanilla ice cream
- 85 ml whole milk
- 4 Oreo cookies
- Whipped cream, for topping
- Crushed Oreo cookies, for garnish

Instruction:

1. Add vanilla ice cream, whole milk, and Oreo cookies to the empty container in the order listed.
2. Follow the quick instructions for assembly and processing.
3. Select the MILKSHAKE program.
4. Once processing is complete, add whipped cream on top.
5. Garnish with crushed Oreo cookies.
6. Serve immediately.

Per Serving:

Calories: 480; Fat: 25g;
Carbohydrates: 56g; Protein: 8g

Coconut Milkshake

Serves: 1 ; Prep: 5 Min

Ingredient

- 200g vanilla ice cream
- 85 ml whole milk
- 50 ml coconut milk
- 1 tablespoon shredded coconut
- Whipped cream, for topping (optional)
- Toasted coconut flakes, for garnish (optional)

Instruction:

1. Add vanilla ice cream, whole milk, coconut milk, and shredded coconut to the empty container in the order listed.
2. Follow the quick instructions for assembly and processing.
3. Select the MILKSHAKE program.
4. Once processing is complete, add whipped cream on top if desired.
5. Garnish with toasted coconut flakes.
6. Serve immediately.

Per Serving:

Calories: 480; Fat: 32g;
Carbohydrates: 41g; Protein: 7g

CHAPTER 06: MILKSHAKE

Coffee Milkshake

Serves: 1 ; Prep: 5 Min

Ingredient

- 200g vanilla ice cream
- 85 ml whole milk
- 60 ml brewed coffee, chilled
- 1 tablespoon chocolate syrup
- Whipped cream, for topping (optional)
- Chocolate shavings, for garnish (optional)

Instruction:

1. Add vanilla ice cream, whole milk, chilled brewed coffee, and chocolate syrup to the empty container in the order listed.
2. Follow the quick instructions for assembly and processing.
3. Select the MILKSHAKE program.
4. Once processing is complete, add whipped cream on top if desired.
5. Garnish with chocolate shavings.
6. Serve immediately.

Per Serving:

Calories: 380; Fat: 20g;
Carbohydrates: 44g; Protein: 6g

Blueberry Milkshake

Serves: 1 ; Prep: 5 Min

Ingredient

- 200g vanilla ice cream
- 85 ml whole milk
- 100 g fresh blueberries
- 1 tablespoon honey or sugar (optional)
- Whipped cream, for topping (optional)

Per Serving:

Calories: 340; Fat: 18g;
Carbohydrates: 40g; Protein: 5g

Instruction:

1. Add vanilla ice cream, whole milk, fresh blueberries, and honey or sugar (if using) to the empty container in the order listed.
2. Follow the quick instructions for assembly and processing.
3. Select the MILKSHAKE program.
4. Once processing is complete, add whipped cream on top if desired.
5. Serve immediately.

CHAPTER 06: MILKSHAKE

Peach Milkshake

Serves: 1 ; Prep: 5 Min

Ingredient

- 200g vanilla ice cream
- 85 ml whole milk
- 150g fresh ripe peaches, pitted and sliced
- 1 tablespoon honey or sugar (optional)

Per Serving:

Calories: 320; Fat: 17g;
Carbohydrates: 38g; Protein: 5g

Instruction:

1. Add vanilla ice cream, whole milk, fresh peaches, and honey or sugar (if using) to the empty container in the order listed.
2. Follow the quick instructions for assembly and processing.
3. Select the MILKSHAKE program.
4. Once processing is complete, serve immediately.

Raspberry Milkshake

Serves: 1 ; Prep: 5 Min

Ingredient

- 200g vanilla ice cream
- 85 ml whole milk
- 100g fresh raspberries
- 1 tablespoon honey or sugar (optional)

Instruction:

1. Add vanilla ice cream, whole milk, fresh raspberries, and honey or sugar (if using) to the empty container in the order listed.
2. Follow the quick instructions for assembly and processing.
3. Select the MILKSHAKE program.
4. Once processing is complete, serve immediately.

Per Serving:

Calories: 250; Fat: 12g;
Carbohydrates: 32g; Protein: 5g

CHAPTER 06: MILKSHAKE

Cherry Milkshake

Serves: 1 ; Prep: 5 Min

Ingredient

- 200g vanilla ice cream
- 85 ml whole milk
- 100g fresh cherries, pitted
- 1 tablespoon honey or sugar (optional)

Instruction:

1. Add vanilla ice cream, whole milk, fresh cherries, and honey or sugar (if using) to the empty container in the order listed.
2. Follow the quick instructions for assembly and processing.
3. Select the MILKSHAKE program.
4. Once processing is complete, serve immediately.

Per Serving:

Calories: 280; Fat: 12g;
Carbohydrates: 38g; Protein: 6g

Nutella Milkshake

Serves: 1 ; Prep: 5 Min

Ingredient

- 200g vanilla ice cream
- 85 ml whole milk
- 2 tablespoons Nutella hazelnut spread

Instruction:

1. Add vanilla ice cream, whole milk, and Nutella hazelnut spread to the empty container in the order listed.
2. Follow the quick instructions for assembly and processing.
3. Select the MILKSHAKE program.
4. Once processing is complete, serve immediately.

Per Serving:

Calories: 440; Fat: 24g;
Carbohydrates: 48g; Protein: 8g

CHAPTER 06: MILKSHAKE

Almond Joy Milkshake

Serves: 1 ; Prep: 5 Min

Ingredient

- 200g vanilla ice cream
- 85 ml whole milk
- 2 tablespoons chocolate syrup
- 1 tablespoon shredded coconut
- 1 tablespoon sliced almonds

Instruction:

1. Add vanilla ice cream, whole milk, chocolate syrup, shredded coconut, and sliced almonds to the empty container in the order listed.
2. Follow the quick instructions for assembly and processing.
3. Select the MILKSHAKE program.
4. Once processing is complete, serve immediately.

Per Serving:

Calories: 490; Fat: 26g;
Carbohydrates: 56g; Protein: 9g

Mocha Milkshake

Serves: 1 ; Prep: 5 Min

Ingredient

- 200g vanilla ice cream
- 85 ml whole milk
- 1 tablespoon instant coffee granules
- 2 tablespoons chocolate syrup

Instruction:

1. Add vanilla ice cream, whole milk, instant coffee granules, and chocolate syrup to the empty container in the order listed.
2. Follow the quick instructions for assembly and processing.
3. Select the MILKSHAKE program.
4. Once processing is complete, serve immediately.

Per Serving:

Calories: 350; Fat: 15g;
Carbohydrates: 45g; Protein: 7g

CHAPTER 06: MILKSHAKE

Caramel Macchiato Milkshake

Serves: 1 ; Prep: 5 Min

Ingredient

- 200g vanilla ice cream
- 85 ml whole milk
- 1 tablespoon instant coffee granules
- 2 tablespoons caramel sauce

Instruction:

1. Add vanilla ice cream, whole milk, instant coffee granules, and caramel sauce to the empty container in the order listed.
2. Follow the quick instructions for assembly and processing.
3. Select the MILKSHAKE program.
4. Once processing is complete, serve immediately.

Per Serving:

Calories: 380; Fat: 16g;
Carbohydrates: 52g; Protein: 7g

Key Lime Pie Milkshake

Serves: 1 ; Prep: 5 Min

Ingredient

- 200g vanilla ice cream
- 85 ml whole milk
- 2 tablespoons key lime juice
- 1 tablespoon sweetened condensed milk
- 2 graham crackers, crushed

Instruction:

1. Add vanilla ice cream, whole milk, key lime juice, and sweetened condensed milk to the empty container in the order listed.
2. Follow the quick instructions for assembly and processing.
3. Select the MILKSHAKE program.
4. Once processing is complete, add crushed graham crackers to the milkshake.
5. Serve immediately.

<u>Per Serving:</u>

Calories: 380; Fat: 16g; Carbohydrates: 52g; Protein: 7g

CHAPTER 06: MILKSHAKE

Pineapple Coconut Milkshake

Serves: 1 ; Prep: 5 Min

Ingredient

- 200g vanilla ice cream
- 85 ml whole milk
- 100g fresh pineapple chunks
- 2 tablespoons shredded coconut

Instruction:

1. Add vanilla ice cream, whole milk, fresh pineapple chunks, and shredded coconut to the empty container in the order listed.
2. Follow the quick instructions for assembly and processing.
3. Select the MILKSHAKE program.
4. Once processing is complete, remove the milkshake from the tub and serve immediately.

<u>Per Serving:</u>

Calories: 380; Fat: 18g; Carbohydrates: 50g; Protein: 6g

Mango Milkshake

Serves: 1 ; **Prep: 5 Min**

Ingredient

- 200g vanilla ice cream
- 85 ml whole milk
- 150g fresh ripe mango, peeled and diced

Instruction:

1. Add vanilla ice cream, whole milk, and fresh diced mango to the empty container in the order listed.
2. Follow the quick instructions for assembly and processing.
3. Select the MILKSHAKE program.
4. Once processing is complete, remove the milkshake from the tub and serve immediately.

Per Serving:

Calories: 320; Fat: 14g;
Carbohydrates: 44g; Protein: 5g

CHAPTER 06: MILKSHAKE

Blackberry Milkshake

Serves: 1 ; **Prep: 5 Min**

Ingredient

- 200g vanilla ice cream
- 85 ml whole milk
- 150g fresh blackberries

Instruction:

1. Add vanilla ice cream, whole milk, and fresh blackberries to the empty container in the order listed.
2. Follow the quick instructions for assembly and processing.
3. Select the MILKSHAKE program.
4. Once processing is complete, remove the milkshake from the tub and serve immediately.

Per Serving:

Calories: 280; Fat: 12g;
Carbohydrates: 38g; Protein: 4g

Make one-of-a-kind treats
with extracts & mix-ins

1. Make a base

Start by making any base from this guide & add an extract if desired.

To make even more flavours, substitute vanilla extract with 1 teaspoon of fruit, herb or nut extract.

2. Freeze

Cover with lid and freeze for 24 hours

3. Process

Select the program that matches your base
ICE CREAM
GELATO
LIGHT ICE CREAM

4. Add mix-ins

With a spoon, create a 4cm wide hole that reaches the bottom of the tub. Add your mix-ins to the hole in the tub.

5. Process

Press MIX-IN program.

Don't want to wait? Scoop in some shop-bought ice cream into the tub and skip to step 4.

Mix-in

Mix in chocolate, nuts, sweets, fruit and more to elevate any treat with bursts of flavour

Hard mix-ins
will remain intact.
Mix-ins like chocolate, sweets and nuts will not be broken down during the MIX-IN program. We recommend using mini chocolate chips, mini sweets or pre-chopped ingredients.

Soft mix-ins
will get broken down.
Mix-ins like cookies and frozen fruit will end up smaller after the MIX-IN program. We recommend using bigger pieces of soft ingredients

FOR ICE CREAM & GELATO ONLY

We don't recommend
fresh fruit, sauces and spreads to use as mix-ins.
Adding fresh fruit, fudge and caramel sauces will soften your treat. Chocolate hazelnut spread and nut butters generally do not incorporate well. We recommend using frozen fruit or chocolate/caramel shell toppings with the mix-in program and only enjoying sauces and spreads as toppings

Creative with mix-ins

Mint Chocolate Chip	Strawberry	Chocolate Caramel Nut Cluster
Base: Vanilla (leave out vanilla extract) **Extract:** 1 tsp peppermint extract (Add green food colouring, optional) **Mix-in:** 45g mini chocolate chips	**Base:** Strawberry **Extract:** N/A **Mix-in:** 2 tbsp freeze dried strawberries or strawberry flakes	**Base:** Vanilla **Extract:** N/A **Mix-in:** 45g chocolate covered caramel sweets (broken), 2 tablespoons roasted hazelnuts (broken)
Sundae Cone	**Death by Chocolate**	**Banana Chocolate Chunk**
Base: Vanilla **Extract:** N/A **Mix-in:** 1 tbsp chocolate shell topping, 2 tbsp peanuts, 2 tbsp sugar cone pieces	**Base:** Chocolate **Extract:** N/A **Mix-in:** 2 tbsp mini chocolate chips, 2 tbsp brownie bits	**Base:** Vanilla, Chocolate **Extract:** N/A **Mix-in:** 1 tbsp banana chips, broken into pieces, 2 tbsp chocolate chips
Chocolate Chip Cookie Dough	**Chocolate Cookies & Cream**	**Orange Cream**
Base: Vanilla **Extract:** N/A **Mix-in:** 45g edible frozen cookie dough chunks + 1 tbsp mini chocolate chips	**Base:** Chocolate **Extract:** N/A **Mix-in:** 3 chocolate sandwich biscuits, broken	**Base:** Vanilla (leave out vanilla extract) **Extract:** 1 tsp orange extract **Mix-in:** N/A
Rum Raisin	**Lemon Vanilla**	**Salted Caramel**
Base: Vanilla **Extract:** N/A **Mix-in:** 40g raisins (soaked in 1 tsp rum)	**Base:** Vanilla (leave out vanilla extract) **Extract:** 1 tsp lemon extract **Mix-in:** N/A	**Base:** Chocolate **Extract:** N/A **Mix-in:** 2 tbsp salted caramel

Manufactured by Amazon.ca
Bolton, ON